HOW TO TEACH SO STUDENTS
REMEMBER

2ND EDITION

ASCD MEMBER BOOK

Many ASCD members received this book as a
member benefit upon its initial release.

Learn more at: **www.ascd.org/memberbooks**

MARILEE **SPRENGER**

HOW TO TEACH SO STUDENTS REMEMBER

2ND EDITION

Alexandria, Virginia USA

1703 N. Beauregard St. • Alexandria, VA 22311-1714 USA
Phone: 800-933-2723 or 703-578-9600 • Fax: 703-575-5400
Website: www.ascd.org • E-mail: member@ascd.org
Author guidelines: www.ascd.org/write

Deborah S. Delisle, *Executive Director;* Stefani Roth, *Publisher;* Genny Ostertag, *Director, Content Acquisitions;* Carol Collins, *Senior Acquisitions Editor;* Julie Houtz, *Director, Book Editing & Production;* Liz Wegner, *Editor;* Georgia Park, *Senior Graphic Designer;* Mike Kalyan, *Director, Production Services;* Keith Demmons, *Production Designer;* Kelly Marshall, *Senior Production Specialist*

PAPERBACK ISBN: 978-1-4166-2531-5   ASCD product #118016
PDF E-BOOK ISBN: 978-1-4166-2532-2; see Books in Print for other formats.
Quantity discounts are available: e-mail programteam@ascd.org or call 800-933-2723, ext. 5773, or 703-575-5773. For desk copies, go to www.ascd.org/deskcopy.

ASCD Member Book No. FY18-5 (Feb. 2018 P). ASCD Member Books mail to Premium (P), Select (S), and Institutional Plus (I+) members on this schedule: Jan, PSI+; Feb, P; Apr, PSI+; May, P; Jul, PSI+; Aug, P; Sep, PSI+; Nov, PSI+; Dec, P. For current details on membership, see www.ascd.org/membership.

Library of Congress Cataloging-in-Publication Data

Names: Sprenger, Marilee, 1949- author.
Title: How to teach so students remember / Marilee Sprenger.
Description: Second Edition. | Alexandria, Virginia : ASCD, [2018] | Includes
    bibliographical references and index.
Identifiers: LCCN 2017048994 (print) | LCCN 2017051027 (ebook) | ISBN
    9781416625322 (PDF) | ISBN 9781416625315 (paperback)
Subjects: LCSH: Teaching. | Learning. | Memory.
Classification: LCC LB1027 (ebook) | LCC LB1027 .S685 2018 (print) | DDC
    371.102--dc23
LC record available at https://lccn.loc.gov/2017048994

27 26 25 24 23 22 21 20 19 18   1 2 3 4 5 6 7 8 9 10 11 12

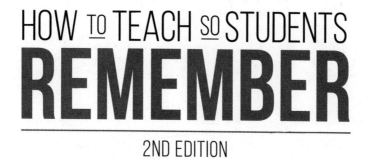

HOW TO TEACH SO STUDENTS
REMEMBER

2ND EDITION

Acknowledgments

An incredible group of friends, researchers, and colleagues invested much time and energy in this book.

Many memory researchers are working diligently to find answers to the various questions we all have about how our memories work. I want to thank Daniel Schacter for his research and his wonderful publications, for the time he devoted to examining the seven steps, and for his encouragement. The work done by such influencers as Robert Marzano, Eric Jensen, David Sousa, John Hattie, Rick Wormeli, and many others has contributed greatly to the pursuit of higher student achievement. We are all better-informed educators as a result.

I am grateful to the people at ASCD, especially Carol Collins, Stefani Roth, Genny Ostertag, and Liz Wegner, for their support, encouragement, and cooperation.

I am indebted to all "my kids"—the students who have taught me so much—and to the thousands of teachers whose lives have touched mine.

As always, I want to thank my husband, who adjusts to my schedules, carries my luggage, and offers me unconditional support.

Introduction to
the Second Edition

**Learning is how we acquire information, and memory
is how we store that information. Education is about
enhancing learning, and neuroscience is about
trying to understand how learning and memory
occur. Memory is the glue that binds our
mental life together.**

—*Eric Kandel*

It is exciting to be writing a second edition of *How to Teach So Students
Remember*. Neuroscientists are working hard to find more strategies to help
today's teachers, who can rightly be called brain-changers, dendrite growers,
or even neuroeducators. Because the brain exhibits plasticity, the experiences
students have in the classroom can and will create neurological changes.

Among the most important changes to students' brains are those related
to memory. We are constantly accessing prior knowledge—long-term memory
—to make sense of our world. We take in new information through our
sensory memory, hold onto it through working memory, and place it in long-
term memory for later use. All this happens through electrical and chemical
connections.

One researcher whose work on memory I've always been in awe of is
Dan Schacter, author of the books *Searching for Memory* (1996) and *The Seven
Sins of Memory* (2001). Schacter was the man I decided to contact when I
woke up in the middle of the night with the idea to break teaching down

1

for memory into seven distinct steps. Why seven? Because the more we can chunk learning down for students, the less strain we place on their working memory, which can't work properly if it's spilling over with information. When working memory can't work, long-term memory can't store information; it is the connection between these two processes that creates memories.

Think about how you have learned things in the past. Perhaps you have recently learned to play golf, speak a foreign language, or use a new digital device. Amazingly, the likelihood is that you'd use the exact same process to learn all three—and just about anything else.

First, you made a conscious decision to learn something. For some reason this idea grabbed you, and you reached for it. You found out about it, you thought about it, decided on the program you would use to learn it, and began to take in information about it. Your coach or instructor gave you information that you had to put into your own words. You received feedback on your understanding thus far. You made corrections as necessary and continued learning through practicing. As you made improvements, you planned how you would use the new information or skill. You set a date to try it out, ensuring to conduct one last review beforehand. When the time came to show your skill, you searched your memory for the right words or actions. Because you practiced so much, your memory did not fail you and you achieved your goal by mastering what you needed to. Through the learning process, you climbed the following seven steps:

Step 1: Reach and Teach. You discovered or were motivated to learn something and began your learning.

Research has shown us that we must engage students if they are to retain information effectively (Marzano, Pickering, & Heflebower, 2010). To this end, our classrooms must be student-centered rather than teacher-centered. Personalized learning, problem-based learning, project-based learning, and inquiry learning are some popular ways of ensuring that lessons are student-centered. Because information is received through sensory memory, we are prudent to consider novelty, need, choice, attention, motivation, emotion, and meaning when designing learning experiences.

Step 2: Reflect. You thought about what you were doing and what it meant in your life.

There's an old joke about teaching being an instructor's ability to transfer her notes to the student's notebook without having them pass through either one's brain. In some cases, I believe that students can take notes robotically and not think at all about the material being presented. Giving students time to "linger over learning" (Rogers, 2013) may help them make the connections from new material to old. This working memory process can lead to higher-level thinking.

Step 3: Recode. You put your new knowledge into words so your coach or instructor knew that you had learned it.

Recoding is a way to organize information in the brain at many levels—an imperative step for memory retention. Students must take information and make it their own. Using working memory and accessing prior knowledge through long-term memory allow learners to put information into their own words, pictures, sounds, or movements. Material that is self-generated in this way is better recalled. The recoded material has become a memory and triggers conceptual understanding.

Step 4: Reinforce. You received feedback from your coach letting you know whether to backtrack and relearn or move on.

From the recoding process, teachers can discover whether student perceptions match their expectations. Through feedback loops, concepts and processes may be perfected. Motivational feedback, informational feedback, or developmental feedback may be desirable. This step offers teachers the opportunity to catch misconceptions before they become long-term memories that are difficult to change.

Step 5: Rehearse. You practiced, practiced, practiced.

Both rote rehearsal and elaborative rehearsal have their place in putting information into long-term, permanent memory. Rehearsing in different ways involves higher levels of thinking, including applying, analyzing, and creating. Developing strategies for rehearsal and the spacing effect will help teachers and students discover optimal rehearsal techniques. Sleep is also essential in establishing long-term memories.

Step 6: Review. Before showing off your new talent, you went over what you had learned.

Whereas rehearsal puts information into long-term memory, review allows learners to retrieve that information and manipulate it in working memory. The products of the manipulation can then be returned to long-term memory. As we prepare our students for high-stakes testing, we must match our instruction, review, and assessment procedures to give them the greatest opportunity for achievement. Review must also include test-taking skills.

Step 7: Retrieve. When using your new knowledge, you were able to access the memory you developed through learning.

The type of assessment used can affect the student's ability to retrieve stored information. Accessing stored memories may be reliant on specific cues. The retrieval process may also be triggered through recognition techniques, as well as recall. Stress can inhibit the ability to access memories and must also be addressed.

In this book, I take these seven steps and chunk them down so that any teacher can follow the process. Some of the steps you have used often in many lessons, but a few—reflection, recoding, and reinforcement—are sometimes overlooked. The following chapters describe how to develop these steps, how to access higher levels of thinking, and how both activities relate to brain activity and brain research. Step by step, we can teach the way the brain learns, take advantage of research-based strategies, and ensure that our students have the ability to transfer information in new and unanticipated circumstances. As students ascend the steps, stronger memories are formed, and higher-level thinking takes place (see Figure I.1).

I have updated this second edition to reflect new knowledge about the brain and memory and new advances in learning, including the following topics and ideas:

- The use of the gradual release of responsibility model, especially for feedback: Imagine students reaching the point where they can provide their own feedback to themselves!
- Recent research on the value of homework: How much and under what circumstances should you assign it?
- New studies on sleep and memory: There is no denying that sleep can make an enormous difference in what kids remember.

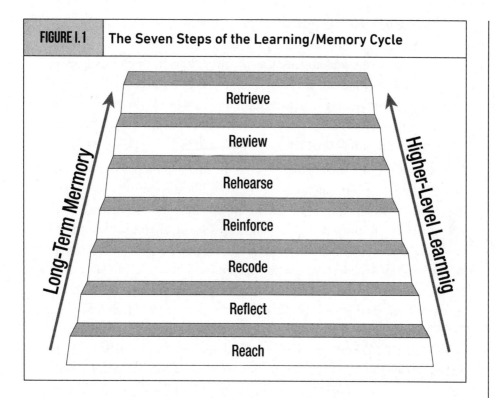

FIGURE I.1 | **The Seven Steps of the Learning/Memory Cycle**

- How movement can optimize memory: Movement builds brains by releasing chemicals to help with focus and long-term retention.
- The latest research on feedback: When should we give it, how often, and in what form?
- A new view of Maslow's hierarchy and the importance of a social brain: What basic student needs must be met for successful learning?
- The importance of a growth mindset: Believing that anyone can learn is paramount to effective teaching.
- Recent research on neurotransmitters: Which ones motivate the brain? How can they be released? How are they affected when goals are achieved?
- Findings from meta-analyses about reviewing: What are some new and effective ways to review content? How should reviewing sessions be spaced out?

- Ways to chunk information: We've been told about chunking for years. Now, let's see how to actually do it!
- New pre-assessment ideas: Can we reach kids through pre-assessment? How should we pre-assess? What do we do with the data?
- New information on metacognition: It's not just thinking about what you thought about—it's thinking while you're thinking! It may sound tricky, but it makes sense.

I've retained the "mental notes" from the first edition of this book, which you will find woven throughout the chapters. Some are direct quotations from current experts on a topic, others are bits of neuroscience findings, and still others are simply scraps of common sense from Grandma, who might as well have been a neuroscientist without the degree. If we had all followed the advice of our wise elders, our brains and our bodies would probably in better shape. If we had played more, moved more, consumed more fruits and vegetables and fewer artificial ingredients, listened more to music and to others, petted more dogs and cats, smiled and laughed every day, and been kinder to ourselves and to others—if we had done all of these simple things our grandparents encouraged us to do, our memories today would be better, our brains would have more connections, we'd have more friends (very good for our brains), and we might have more time on this planet to make things better.

Reflection

Keeping in mind that the reflection process should be encouraged after each step, I end each chapter with a reflection section. If you have not already reflected about what you have read so far, take this opportunity to do so. As you were reading, questions may have come to mind. Think about those questions: Where will you find the answers, and how do they relate to your present situation? If you were taking notes or highlighting, go back over those areas and think about why they may be important to you. Need more information now? Check the references section for further reading, or simply read on!

Reach and Teach

For most of us, our favorite teacher was someone we felt really cared about or challenged us; someone who recognized us and reached out to us.

–*Jonathan Cohen*, Educating Minds and Hearts

I was facing another difficult class of 29 8th graders from a variety of back-grounds. Four of them had been expelled from other schools. Two of them had older brothers who were involved in gang activity. Seventeen came from single-parent homes. Several of them were on welfare. One had a father in prison.

The first day, I had to go over the rules in the handbook. Those who were following along were laughing and making snide remarks—too softly for me to hear exactly what they were saying. I passed out books and collected emergency cards, and finally the day was over.

The second day, I decided to take the students for a "book walk" through the social studies text. I had read recently that pre-exposure to the material would help students feel more comfortable later when we cover it. Two students started a verbal battle over some of the content. Fifteen others joined in. My room was next to the principal's office, and I feared the ruckus could be overheard. My heart was racing. I looked at the clock, praying it was time for the bell. No such luck. I wondered how teachers on television and in movies could always be "saved by the bell." I opened my desk drawer and pulled out a whistle. One quick blow and the kids quieted down. Some were surprised, others angry, but quiet. I gave them a quick assign-ment: to draw a picture of any historical event they wanted. I sat and waited for the class to end.

The bell rang, and I beat the students out the door. On my way out, I literally run into one of my colleagues. I looked him in the eye and said, "I cannot teach these kids!"

He looked back at me and responded, "Sure you can—but first, you have to get their attention. If you can't do that, you can get a different job."

I was taken aback, but I knew he was right. I started thinking about how I was able to reach students in the other classes I'd taught. I knew the whistle worked only because it was novel. Should I come up with other novel ideas? What else might be valuable? To reach my students, I would definitely need to get their attention. I would also need to forge emotional connections and good working relationships with them. I would need to understand their learning preferences, and I would need to make the material relevant to their lives.

Stimuli, Attention, and Learning

We are bombarded with sensory stimuli throughout the day: 2,000 bits of information are allowed in by the brain's filtering system every second (Willis, 2009/2010). According to neuroscientist Michael Gazzaniga (1999), our brain retains only about 1 percent of that information. How do we help our students hold onto even the sensory information, let alone all the semantic information they need to remember? According to Shaun Kerry (2002) of the American Board of Psychiatry and Neurology, whether certain events or information are retained in memory is "dependent upon an individual's love for the subject matter and its dramatic, emotional, auditory, and visual impact."

I used to always consider "attention" only in the context of attention spans. How long could I keep students' attention before their minds drifted away? The formula I'd learned was that attention spans are equal to students' ages in minutes. So, for example, a 7-year-old student has a seven-minute attention span.

Before students can even have an attention span for learning, they must train their attention on the information at hand. Consider the following scenario:

It is time for Writer's Workshop. The 3rd graders are scattered throughout the room. There is a low buzz of conversation as some of the students discuss their writing with others. The teacher is conferencing with J.D.

Katie sits quietly at a desk, rereading her short essay on her favorite book. As she reads, she pauses to draw a picture depicting an episode in the book. Jamie approaches Katie's desk and asks to borrow a blue marker. Katie stops reading and hands the marker to her. Jamie glances at the picture Katie is drawing and asks her several questions about the book. Katie colors in the house she has drawn as she describes the characters and the scene. Interrupting the conversation, Angelo says he needs to get a book out of the desk at which Katie is seated. He excuses himself and starts looking for the book. Katie must stand now to color while she carries on her account to Jamie.

Katie keeps coloring with her right hand while using her left hand to grab the book she has spotted for Angelo, who thanks her and goes back to the table where students are peer editing. Jamie's interest is piqued by Katie's account of the story, so she asks for the name of the book author. Katie has loaned the book to Tiffany, who sits across the aisle, so the girls ask Tiffany who the author is, maintaining their dialogue as they await a response. Katie is listening to Jamie's comment about the book as she admires the picture she drew. She is also listening for Tiffany's voice to tell her the author's name. Katie picks up a green marker and draws a large tree next to the house as Tiffany reads the author's name and Jamie returns to her seat.

Brain research suggests that there are four essential criteria for gaining attention: *need, novelty, meaning,* and *emotion* (Tate, 2016). Attention itself, according to Andreason (2004), is the cognitive process that allows Katie to ignore irrelevant stimuli (extraneous student conversations), notice important stimuli (her essay, her picture, Jamie's comments), and shift from one stimulus to another (from talking to Jamie to drawing the picture, from interacting with Angelo to interacting with Jamie and Tiffany). She was balancing visual information in the picture. She attends to auditory information as she listens to Jamie and for Tiffany. The tactile information she is dealing with includes drawing her picture, grabbing the book for Angelo, and giving Jamie the marker.

Andreason divides attention into five types: *sustained, directed, selective, divided,* and *focused*:

- *Sustained* attention involves focusing for a long period of time. Creating lesson plans or assessments requires this type of attention.
- *Directed* attention occurs when we consciously select a particular stimulus from all that bombards us. This is the attention we give students who disrupt the class, for example.
- *Selective* attention involves focusing on one particular stimulus for a personal or sensible reason. For instance, a student may select to listen to a whisper from another student rather than to the lecture being given.
- *Divided* attention occurs as we rapidly shift focus from one thing to another. Our students are dealing with divided attention when they do their homework in front of the television.
- *Focused* attention is directed to a particular aspect of some stimulus. When we ask students to focus on the answer to an essential question as they research on the internet, we are asking them to engage in this kind of attention.

Attention is necessary for thinking. The brain scans the environment, sifting through sensory messages to find something to pay attention to. The brain is always attending; our students just may not be attending to what we desire.

The Biological Basis for Attention

Attention requires three elements: *arousal, orientation,* and *focus* (McNeil, 2009). The reticular activating system in our brains (see Appendix A) controls *arousal* levels through the amount of neurotransmission it emits. Stimulation of the frontal lobes by norepinephrine and dopamine changes the brain's electrical activity and causes us to be alert, at which point the parietal lobe disengages from the current stimulus, and we are *oriented* to the new stimulus. The thalamus then controls the situation and allows us to *focus* as it carries the new information to the frontal lobes. The thalamus has the power to inhibit other sensory stimulation to aid us. The anterior cingulate allows us to maintain attention (McNeil, 2009). The hippocampus is a major player in the attention process. Because of its access to so many memories, if the reticular activating system reacts to some sensory stimulation, the hippocampus can compare it to old experiences and determine its novelty (Ratey, 2008).

This biological information confirms to us that the attention process can be aided by instruction—the anterior cingulates of students will focus on whatever we, the teachers, bring to their attention. Consider the following example:

Noah is playing on his tablet. It is seven o'clock, but he is too engrossed in his game to realize that time is passing quickly. His tablet suddenly goes dead. Noah had received a warning that the battery was low, but he wouldn't stop the game to find his charger. With the battery completely dead, he searches through his room to find the cord and plugs it in. While waiting for enough of a charge to continue his game, Noah glances at the clock. He can't believe time slipped by so quickly.

Noah's reticular activating system arouses him. He has a load of homework to complete and obviously didn't realize how time flies!

Noah looks at his stack of books. He begins to prioritize. "Let's see. I might be able to get my English done on the bus tomorrow. I have to finish my math now because I might need Mom's help. Then I'd better practice those words for my spelling test."

Noah's frontal lobes are now orienting him to his homework. They are helping him plan and prioritize. He "needs" his mom to help with math, which is why that subject gets his attention.

Noah pulls his math book from the pile, opens his notebook, and is completely focused on his work. He doesn't hear his mom open the door to look in on him.

Noah's thalamus has filtered out sensory stimuli that will not aid him in his current focus of attention, his math homework.

> ☀ **Mental Note: Without awareness of incoming information, explicit learning cannot occur.**

Motivation and Meaning

Jeremy and Joe are good friends. They've attended school together since kindergarten. Their mothers belong to the same book club, and their fathers often golf together.

On this sunny Saturday afternoon, Jeremy and Joe are going to the batting cages. Baseball season is right around the corner, and they're hoping to move from the junior varsity team to varsity. They are just gathering their bats when Joe's dad approaches.

"Hey, guys, how about coming to the course with us this afternoon? We could use some good caddies," he asks.

Jeremy's face immediately lights up. "That sounds like fun. I could use some pointers on my golf game, and it's really a great day to be out in the sunshine! Don't you think so, Joe? We can go to the cages afterward. You've been saying you want to try out for the golf team. This could be a great opportunity."

Joe, however, is not convinced. When his dad looks at him for a reply and sees the negative look on his face, he sighs and says, "OK, Joe, we'll pay you for your trouble."

Joe nods his head. "OK, but it has to be more than 10 bucks. That's what you gave me last time—I won't do it for that."

Two similar boys with similar interests, yet quite different responses: Whereas Joe required *extrinsic* motivation—money—to caddy, Jeremy was happy to do it for *intrinsic* reasons. For Jeremy, the prospect of caddying includes at least three of the four criteria for capturing attention suggested by the research: need (he "could use some pointers"), meaning (it's a way to bond with his friend and their dads in fine weather), and emotion (he takes pleasure out of the game).

Why We Do the Things We Do

Merriam-Webster (2003) defines *motive* as "something (as a need or desire) that causes a person to act" (p. 759). When I ask my students about their needs, they usually oblige with a very long list that nevertheless excludes the content I teach them! Students too often do not see reading, math, history, science, or writing as a necessity. It's up to us as teachers to prove to them that the topics are necessary and even desirable to learn.

Intrinsic motivation comes from within—it is a desire or need that the brain determines is pleasurable or important. When we are intrinsically motivated, neurotransmitters such as dopamine and norepinephrine are released in our brains (Burns, 2012). These chemicals provide the "get up and go" necessary for us to accomplish our goals. The same neurotransmitters are released anew when our goal is attained. Dopamine, the pleasure chemical, makes us want to achieve goals again to repeat the good feeling.

Extrinsic motivation, by contrast, is associated with rewards and punishment. Some researchers, such as Alfie Kohn (1993), believe that extrinsic motivators can alter the brain to shift a goal from attaining the nominal objective to either attaining some tangible reward or avoiding a punishment. If dopamine is released when students receive rewards, their brains may become trained to associate the resulting good feeling with the rewards rather than the accomplishments.

In our sample scenario, Jeremy is seeking his feel-good neurotransmitters from the experience and the learning, whereas Joe seeks his from the payment. Many researchers believe that the external reward must get larger to receive the same level of pleasure or excitement over time. This is why Joe won't settle for $10 anymore.

Mental Note: Attention and motivation require need, novelty, meaning, or emotion.

Maslow's Hierarchy

According to Abraham Maslow's hierarchy of needs (see Figure 1.1), certain needs must be met before the brain can focus on academic achievement. Maslow's hierarchy begins with physiological needs and proceeds upward through safety, belonging, esteem, and, finally, self-actualization (Maslow & Lowery, 1998):

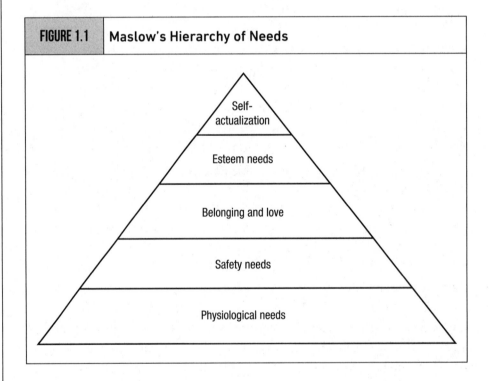

FIGURE 1.1 Maslow's Hierarchy of Needs

Self-actualization

Esteem needs

Belonging and love

Safety needs

Physiological needs

- **Physiological needs.** These consist of basic survival requirements. Food, water, shelter, and clothing fall into this category. If a student is hungry, that hunger will remain the student's first priority until it is satisfied. Attention will always be focused on unmet needs.
- **Safety needs.** Security, freedom from threat, and predictability are all important to the brain's need for safety. If physiological needs are met, the brain focuses on the safety needs. Once these are met, it turns itself

toward the next level. If our students feel safe and unthreatened in our classrooms, their levels of focus and attention are not impeded.

- **Belonging and love.** These two needs taken together are a primary motivator for the brain. People seek to overcome loneliness when their physical needs have been met and they feel safe. Relationships with friends, spouses, and children provide a sense of belonging. Students who have good relationships with their teachers and other students have neurotransmitters such as serotonin and dopamine released in their brains to make them feel good and feel motivated.
- **Esteem needs.** Self-respect, achievement and success, and a good reputation fall into this category. Feeling valuable in the classroom helps our students focus. Especially when they feel valuable to the teacher, they put forth more effort.
- **Self-actualization.** This level is defined as becoming what the individual is most suited for. Attaining this highest level on the hierarchy is an incredible accomplishment that we want for all of our students. They must first know that they are safe, that they belong and are valued, and that they can respect themselves as others respect them.

Lieberman's View of Basic Needs

Neuroscientist Matthew Lieberman (2013) believes that Maslow had it wrong! Because we are born totally dependent on others for food, shelter, and so on, Lieberman has inverted Maslow's hierarchy somewhat (see Figure 1.2). In his view, social ostracism can be just as devastating as physical pain, so it follows that the strongest need is for social acceptance.

In our students' world, belonging to a social group can take precedence over hunger and other basic needs. For example, my 7th grader Kakisha almost wet her pants once because she would not go to the restroom until the girls divided themselves into teams for volleyball, afraid that she wouldn't get chosen if she weren't around.

To reach our students, we must be aware of their needs and make every effort to meet them so they will be able to attend to the information we want them to learn and remember.

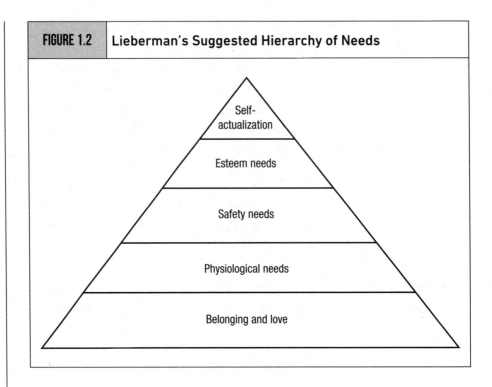

FIGURE 1.2   Lieberman's Suggested Hierarchy of Needs

Self-actualization

Esteem needs

Safety needs

Physiological needs

Belonging and love

Glasser's Choice Theory of Motivation

In his book *Choice Theory*, William Glasser (1999) defines five equally important needs: survival, belonging and love, power, freedom, and fun. On the cover of his book is a statement that epitomizes this theory: "Choosing the life you want and staying close to the people you need."

From his theory, we can conclude that offering choices to our students (that is, responding to their needs for power and freedom) may also make them feel good about what they are doing and therefore make them more motivated and attentive. Belonging and love encompass the latter part of the statement. Students need to feel close to others and know that they can rely on their teachers and their peers.

According to Brophy (1987), student motivation is an acquired competence developed "through general experience, but it is stimulated through modeling, communication of expectations, and direct instruction or socialization by significant others" (p. 41). Therefore, the classroom environment—how the teacher affects the socialization process, what the expectations are and how they are communicated, and the modeling component—can significantly influence student motivation and attention.

> ☀ **Mental Note: The brain cannot focus on learning if basic needs are not met; students may define basic needs differently than we do.**

How Emotions Affect Learning

Vanessa is in the school storeroom gathering material for an art project. Art is not her favorite subject, and her selection shows little creative effort. She has collected markers, paper, and rulers. Nothing is sparking ideas for the assignment called "My Ideal Spot." Vanessa doesn't want to spend a lot of time on this project because she has two other assignments to complete. As she wanders up one aisle and down another, she spots Jessie. Jessie is a student who does it all. She takes ballet and piano, writes award-winning essays, and is very artistic. She loves projects like this. Jessie is bright and lets others know it.

Vanessa notices Jessie's acquisitions. She has filled her arms with glue, glitter, cotton, clay, and oil paint. Vanessa turns to avoid Jessie, who will undoubtedly brag about her project, but it's too late. Jessie walks up to Vanessa and looks at her meager collection of items. She smiles and pushes her heavy load toward Vanessa. She glances down at the markers and asks, "You just getting started?"

Vanessa feels totally inadequate and replies, "Yes, I just got here and grabbed some of the usuals. Now I'm backtracking to get the good stuff."

"So, what's your project going to be?" Jessie asks. Vanessa suspects that she is just asking so she can outdo her with a fabulous project idea.

Vanessa tries to think quickly and responds with, "Oh, my ideal spot is a secret place that I share with my friends. I have to check with them and make sure it's OK to use it for this project." Vanessa thinks that should quiet Jessie down. After all, she probably doesn't have a spot she shares with friends!

"Well, my ideal spot is in Hawaii," Jessie says. "My family goes there every year for two weeks. There are wonderful beaches, and there's an awesome volcano. When I told the art teacher about my idea, he was so excited to see it." Jessie rambles on, mentioning plants and places that Vanessa has never heard of. Her mind wanders until she picks up on Jessie's last comment: "Vanessa, if you ever want to learn how to create a fabulous project, let me know."

Vanessa is overcome with anger and embarrassment. She opens her mouth to give Jessie a witty reply, but nothing comes out! Her brain just can't seem to grasp any smart-aleck remarks. She smiles at Jessie with clenched teeth and walks away.

Vanessa is seething. How dare Jessie make a remark like that? "I can do my own art project," she thinks. "I certainly don't need her help. I should have just let her have it, but I'm too much of a lady for that. Why couldn't I think of a comeback? I'm the comeback queen. I always have a comment for everyone."

Vanessa's emotions have her tongue-tied. Goleman (2013) calls this an emotional "hijacking." Higher-level thinking doesn't take place when this phenomenon occurs. Vanessa is stuck in the emotional center of her brain and can't access the creative center. A few hours later, she comes up with several responses for Jessie and even thinks about calling her to share them!

☀ **Mental Note: Engagement is increased when teachers greet students at the beginning of class and say something positive to them.** —*R. Allan Allday, Miranda Bush, Nicole Ticknor, and Lindsay Walker (2011)*

Reaching Students Through Their Emotions

Emotions have a strong influence on learning (Small, 2003). If students are anxious, depressed, or even angry, they do not receive information in an efficient way. The brain is captivated by the emotion and turns attention to it. When these emotions capture the brain's attention, working memory is flooded and cannot work on the task at hand.

Most researchers refer to the six universal emotions: happiness, sadness, fear, anger, surprise, and disgust. These are primary emotions that are found and recognized in all humans all over the world. Secondary emotions are socially oriented; jealousy, guilt, and embarrassment are a few. Finally, some emotions, like tension and well-being, are what Feldman (2007) calls "background emotions."

Emotions are produced in subcortical regions of the brain; they are part of a set of structures that represent body states. Involuntarily engaged, without conscious knowledge, they affect both the brain and the body. Emotions and emotional states are patterns of response that lead to behavior. These emotions and behaviors can occur when people perceive information through the senses or when they conjure up certain memories. The 2015 animated film *Inside Out* portrays quite accurately five core emotions: joy, sadness, fear, anger, and disgust. In the film, the use of these emotions under both difficult and happy times can be easily understood (Desautels, 2016). The emotions Vanessa feels when encountering Jessie represent sensory information and can be rekindled when she thinks of the situation later on. When Vanessa next runs into Jessie, those same emotions may resurface and affect her behavior.

The amygdala is the major player in emotions and their memories. Because the amygdala modulates both explicit and implicit memory as it accesses incoming information, we remember emotionally charged events better than boring or neutral ones (Bloom, Beal, & Kupfer, 2003). According to LeDoux (2002), "Attention, perception, memory, decision making, and the conscious concomitants of each are all swayed in emotional states . . . emotional arousal organizes and coordinates brain activity" (p. 225). In *The Seven Sins of Memory* (2001), Schacter notes that "emotionally charged incidents are better remembered than nonemotional events. The emotional boost begins at the moment that a memory is born, when attention and elaboration strongly influence whether an experience will be subsequently remembered or forgotten" (p. 163).

Stephen Hamann of Emory University uses magnetic resonance imaging (MRI) to gauge emotional responses to words and pictures (Hamann, Ely,

Grafton, & Kilts, 1999). The imaging shows the activation of the amygdala when individuals respond to an emotional sight. "When the amygdala detects emotion, it essentially boosts activity in areas of the brain that form memories," says Hamann. "And that's how it makes a stronger memory and a more vivid memory" (p. 292). Subjects in Hamann's experiments remember twice as many emotional words as neutral ones.

Because emotions are so powerful, incorporating emotion into our teaching is an excellent way to reach our students. If emotion organizes brain activity, and attention and perception are swayed by emotional states, then our everyday experiences in school will become more memorable if we use emotions to reach our students.

Emotional Hooks

Here are some ways to hook students emotionally in the classroom:

- Be sure that your presentation is exciting. Excitatory neurotransmitters are released when we feel excited. Norepinephrine starts a cascade of chemical responses that increase the intensity of the experience and the perception of it.
- Greet students at the beginning of class and say something positive to them (Allday et al., 2011).
- Emotions are contagious (Guillory, Hancock, & Kramer, 2011), so act excited yourself. What excites *you* about what you're teaching?
- Dress in a costume that will garner students' attention—whether approvingly or not!
- Play music that fits the theme of what you are teaching. Music has emotional anchors for many of us. It activates various networks in the brains of our students, including higher-level thinking. (Replaying the music that engaged students in a particular topic at assessment time can also enhance recall.)
- Begin the lesson with a story. This can be a personal story that you somehow relate to the topic at hand, or it can be a secondhand story with connections to the topic. The brain loves stories, as it is a natural way for it to organize information (Willingham, 2004).

- Begin the class by asking students to make a choice. If the issue you will be studying has two sides, divide the room in half and have students choose a side as they enter. Put up two posters, one on each side of the room, to indicate what each side believes.

☀ **Mental Note: Emotions take precedence over all other brain processes.**

Use Advance Organizers to Focus Attention

As Marzano, Pickering, Norford, Paynter, and Gaddy (2001) put it, "We often see what we expect to see" (p. 279). In this way, advance organizers are powerful instruments for focusing our students' attention. These organizers come in many packages. For instance, an advance organizer could be an oral presentation of the subject matter and how it relates to prior knowledge. The most effective graphic organizers focus students by providing them with a framework for learning to which they must adhere.

My favorite organizer is the agree/disagree chart (Burke, 2009; see Figure 1.3). Such a chart is composed of statements that can be presented orally or in writing. I prefer a chart with statements on them and a place to check "agree" or "disagree." The agree/disagree statements will evoke emotions in most students. They also help them understand the concepts that are being shared.

Advance organizers call on prior knowledge. If the students have no previous experience with the subject, you can ask them to make an attempt to agree or disagree. When the unit is nearly finished, I give my students another opportunity to read the statements and agree or disagree. They then compare the original chart with the most recent one. Some students are amazed at what they have learned, while others pat themselves on the back for what they already knew. Most graphic organizers can be used as advance organizers (see Appendix B for several examples).

Here are some other types of graphic organizers that may be helpful:
- *Venn diagrams* help students see similarities and differences.

FIGURE 1.3	Agree/Disagree Chart	Agree	Disagree
1.	Younger people remember more than older people.		
2.	Age has nothing to do with memory.		
3.	Memory is stored in one area of the brain.		
4.	You only have enough immediate memory for a phone number.		
5.	Females have better memories than males.		
6.	You never forget how to ride a bike.		
7.	It is easier to forget than to remember.		
8.	Smells trigger certain memories.		

- *Mind mapping* is a helpful way to organize new material. Recent research has shown it is especially helpful for dyslexic students (Verhoeven & Boersen, 2015).
- *KWHLU charts* help students pay attention: *K* for what you already know, *W* for what you want to know, *H* for how you want to learn it, *L* for what you've learned, and *U* for how you will use what you've learned in your world.
- *Hierarchy diagrams* may be useful for classification purposes.
- *T-charts* can be used to organize many content areas.
- *Sequencing charts* are great for stories or history time frames.

Mental Note: Show the brain what to focus on.

Connecting with Students Through Their Senses

Dividing students into learning "styles" or "preferences" may be helpful for some teachers. When I started on the brain-compatible path to teaching years ago, part of my training was based on the concept that students have preferred modalities of learning. This knowledge changed the way I taught and made my classrooms more "neuro-appropriate." As I saw the effect of continually changing the way in which I presented material and the memory extensions as a result, I always kept in mind three little words: *visual, auditory,* and *kinesthetic.* Today, much research shows that most students are primarily visual in the way they take in information (Medina, 2014). It's easy to see why in our ever-increasingly visual world. We don't have conference calls anymore; instead, we Skype or FaceTime. Students can read textbooks, but it's so much more enjoyable, entertaining, and memorable to learn by watching or listening to the cast album of *Hamilton: An American Musical.*

If we keep in mind that a multisensory approach is going to be much more engaging, we can bypass some of the older ideas about learners. If we remind ourselves that a picture is "worth a thousand words" and use plenty of different kinds of representations, we can keep our classrooms more interesting. And if we never, ever, forget that movement helps the brain in a multitude of ways and keeps our classrooms interesting, we can make a huge difference in the lives of many of our students.

Consider the following example. Students enter my 9th grade classroom on an oppressively warm day. The windows are open, but little air is circulating.

It is time to begin a unit on the Civil War. This is not a favorite topic of mine, perhaps because my own history teacher did a mediocre job of presenting it. With this heat, I am not in the mood to teach at all, let alone approach a challenging topic. I might start the lesson by saying to the kids, "I know you're hot. I am, too. This may be tough, but it's time we started studying the Civil War. Does anyone know anything about that war?"

Alternatively, I might start by playing some appropriate music—maybe "I Wish I Was in Dixie"—and handing students cups of water as they enter the room. When the starting bell rings, I could turn the music off and say, "Walk around the room and look at the Civil War posters and paraphernalia.

As warm as we are today, I want you to realize that the soldiers who fought in this war were wearing heavy uniforms and were out in the sun continuously. How many of you have seen *Gone with the Wind*? Do you remember that there was a lot of bloodshed? I hope that blood doesn't bother you all. It really was a bloody war!"

The second approach to opening the class is more of an attention-getter for several reasons. First, some emotions are evoked with the use of music and the mention of blood. Second, the approach is multisensory: As soon as the students enter the room, they begin moving, listening, and looking. Finally, I relate their present experience of being hot and uncomfortable directly to the individuals we are about to study. I give them water to fulfill a physiological need, as well as to let them know that I understand how they are feeling and that we are in this together.

Mental Note: Although individual learning styles are not truly representative of our students' needs today, teaching in a multisensory fashion can help close the achievement gap.

Relationships

The feeling of togetherness that the second scenario above conveys is only accessible if I have first taken the time to set up relationships with each of my students. This is key to learning in any situation and with people of any age. Our relationships offer a framework for understanding our progress and appreciating the usefulness of what we're learning (Goleman, 2013).

Four emotional intelligence domains can be applied to relationship building in any environment: self-awareness, self-management, social awareness, and relationship management. Self-awareness and self-management deal with *personal skills*. Recognizing our own emotions is critical to attaining the other competencies. If our students know how they feel, they are then able, with guidance, to learn how to manage their emotions. We hope that our students come to school with these abilities, but sometimes it behooves us to add them to our repertoire, as it will make teaching and learning much easier.

By contrast, social awareness and relationship management are *social skills*. Being able to sense others' emotions, understand their perspectives, and show concern can foster powerful teacher–student and student–student relationships in the classroom. Relationship management includes managing conflict, influencing others, and cultivating relationships.

The passions that any of us have for our work may come from pure emotion like excitement, from the satisfaction that we get from the learning, or from the joy of working with others. Any of these motivators activate the left prefrontal cortex, which receives many of those "feel good" neurotransmitters. Simultaneously, the prefrontal circuits quiet feelings of frustration that might interfere with the learning (Goleman, 2013).

Finding Connections

Building relationships with students requires finding common ground with them. The more they feel they are like you or like each other, the more comfortable they are developing relationships that will enhance learning. One method I like to use I borrowed from a 5th grade teacher. It's a get-to-know-each-other activity with a twist (see Figure 1.4). Students receive a sheet divided into boxes to be signed by classmates who meet the criteria stated in each square. They walk around asking others if they like chocolate chip cookies, for example, or if their parents have a red car. They are not allowed simply to shove the sheet in another student's face and say, "Here—sign one." They must approach a fellow student and ask a question pertaining to the sheet. After the sheet is completed, everyone sits down. I then go through each category and ask the students to raise their hands if the category pertains to them. They can look around and see what they have in common with others in the room. The sheets I first use include characteristics that are true of me. The students quickly see what we have in common. A few weeks later, after I've had the opportunity to read personal information about the students that I've asked them to share on index cards, I hand out sheets that feature characteristics or interests that I know students have.

FIGURE 1.4	Get-to-Know-Each-Other Activity

Find someone who. . .		
Has a dog	Has brown eyes	Likes Pepsi more than Coke
Watches *Friends*	Reads a lot	Loves chocolate chip cookies
Has red as a favorite color	Listens to audiobooks	Thinks M&M's are good chocolate
Plays chess	Likes computers	Prefers gold rather than silver
Has a red car	Has two sisters	Is afraid of heights
Travels a lot	Enjoys music	Likes to run
Plays golf	Plays checkers	Has a brother

"A River Runs Through Us" is my all-time favorite relationship-building activity for both the classroom and the staff room. Getting to know one another is as simple as forming a tight circle of chairs. You stand in the middle of the circle and begin by saying something like this: "Hello, my name is _____." The students are instructed to respond, "Hello, _____." Then you say something about yourself, adding "…and a river runs through us"; for example: "I have a dog, and a river runs through us." At this point, any child who has a dog must get up from his or her chair and move to another chair. Quickly, you take one of the empty chairs, leaving one student now in the middle of the circle. The process repeats as before. Try to make sure every child gets a chance to be in the middle. You may have to get back to the middle (which usually happens anyway) and say something that you know pertains to a student who has not had the opportunity to be in the center. By the time this activity concludes (usually about 20 minutes depending on the size of the class), everyone will know each other's names and find things in common with each other. At the end of the first time you do this (students will want to play this game again and again), you may want to say something like, "We all have so many things in common. I believe each and every one of you have similar experiences! A river really does run through us!"

In *The New Art and Science of Teaching*, Robert Marzano (2017) offers the following suggestions for building relationships using both verbal and non-verbal behaviors:

- Greet students at the door.
- Hold informal conferences.
- Attend after-school activities. Your presence at these events will make a difference to your students by showing that you care about them outside of class.
- Give students special responsibilities and leadership roles in class.
- Create a photo bulletin board.
- Hang up students' artwork. Most students like to see their artwork up, even if they say they don't.
- Use gestures and facial expressions to get points across.
- Employ humor. When I taught middle school grammar, two of my favorite phrases to start lessons about punctuation were "Let's eat Grandma" and "The things I love are cooking my family and my friends." Today, with the ubiquity of texting and social media, fewer and fewer people are using standard punctuation on a regular basis.

Social Categories

According to Giannetti and Sagarese (2001), students tend to fall into one of the following four broad social categories:

1. *Popular.* This category often consists of students who are attractive, athletic, and affluent. These students, who often take the lead in deciding what's "in" or "out" among their peers, compose about 35 percent of the student population in the United States. The main emotional issue with this particular group is related to the impermanence of popularity; these kids may be worrying about how to maintain their prized social status.

2. *Fringe.* Students in this category make up about 10 percent of the population. These students sometimes get to hang out with the popular

kids and sometimes don't, rendering them insecure about whether they are popular themselves. Not knowing exactly where they belong is a prominent emotional issue for them.

3. *Friendship Circles*. These are small groups of students who are good friends with one another. They realize they are not popular, but they are content with the companionship. This group makes up roughly 45 percent of the population.

4. *Loners*. This category is composed of the 10 percent or so of kids who have few or no friends. Loners may be bright, ambitious, and years ahead of their peers, or they may have poor social skills and be difficult to be around. Although these students would possibly like to be a part of a group, they are often not accepted. Sometimes these kids may become bitter about their social situation and even lash out.

Giannetti and Sagarese's research suggests that only 45 percent of our students feel confident in their social status at school. The all-too frequent school massacres perpetrated by socially ostracized students should remind us how important it is to be aware of school social structures and their effects on students' emotional stability. One good place to keep aware of things is the school cafeteria at lunchtime, where the dramas of social strata commingling play out as students figure out with whom to sit. To set up strong relationships, all of these students must be able to interact with one another and respect the differences among them.

Empathy

One day, I arrived at school right after the emotional ordeal of having my 9-year-old Sheltie put to sleep by the vet. When I stopped by the office to tell the administrators I was back, my eyes were red from crying. One of my colleagues expressed her sympathy and reminded me, "Don't let those kids see you cry!" I nodded.

Walking despondently down the hall, I began to feel resentful of my coworker's comments. Couldn't I express my emotions? Wouldn't my students think I was heartless if I didn't seem upset? And wouldn't this be an excellent opportunity to teach empathy?

When I arrived at the room, all eyes were on me. "You're here!" exclaimed one of the girls. "Are you sick?" asked another.

"No," I replied. "I just had a very sad experience." I explained what happened.

"My cat had to be put to sleep, Mrs. Sprenger," Nancy offered. "I felt really bad."

"I'm sure you did," I acknowledged.

"It's just a dumb animal," Brett announced.

I looked at Brett, and the students looked at me. "Have you ever had a pet?" I asked.

"Yeah, we got a dog. He sleeps in my room," Brett shared.

The students began to dialogue about loss. Brett sat quietly until the conversation ended. He walked over to me on his way out the door. "I'm sorry, Mrs. S.," he said. "I guess I didn't really think about how it would feel. I'd be upset, just like you."

The students learned two things that day. First, they were able to put themselves in my shoes and understand how I was feeling—what we call *empathy*. Second, they recognized my feelings and saw that I could manage them. According to Comer (2003), "Children need to form emotional bonds with their teachers and see healthy social relationships among the adults in their lives to function well in school" (p. 11).

☀ **Mental Note: Attention and motivation can be directed through personal relationships with students.**

"Why Do I Have to Know This Stuff?"

How many times have we heard this question? When we think about relevance, we can again look at the brain and how it learns and remembers. The brain takes new information and searches long-term memory to find patterns into which it might fit. If you look at Figure 1.5, your brain sees a square. Is it really there? No, but you have a pattern in your brain for squares, and this is what your brain finds to fill in the blanks.

FIGURE 1.5	Searching for a Familiar Pattern

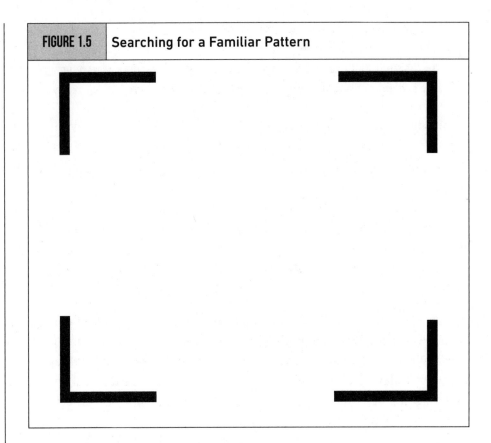

When we offer information to our students, their brains try making connections to already-stored patterns. If there are no connections, the information is easily dropped. Relevancy involves making some associations that affect their lives.

This is not a simple task when we look at the standards and benchmarks that we must reach. Research shows that students perform better when they are provided with criteria, models, and examples that clearly illustrate our expectations (Schmoker, 1999). Student-centered classrooms can be created using both project-based learning and inquiry learning activities that focus on honing information-processing skills and lead to understanding. Reaching our students through relevant issues increases the chances that information will enter the memory process.

Consider which of the following two scenarios you believe would be more appealing to your students:

Scenario 1: Miss Owen's students enter the classroom. They immediately take their seats and get out their notebooks. Today they are studying the Lewis and Clark expedition. They know this because Miss Owen has it written on the whiteboard.

As soon as the bell rings, Miss Owen begins disseminating information via lecture. Some students frantically take notes. Others lose their focus quickly and gaze around the room. Miss Owen has some posters up depicting the events of the expedition. Perhaps some of her students will learn something from the posters.

Scenario 2: Miss Owen's students enter the classroom. On the screen is a picture of a huge mosquito. Beneath the picture is written, "You are part of the Lewis and Clark expedition. One of the biggest nuisances you have are the mosquitoes. They are everywhere. There are times when it is difficult to breathe without inhaling a bug! Research ways to deal with this problem during your expedition. Compare your information with what we would do today." Posters, books, and internet access are available to the students, who are divided into groups.

Miss Owen's students in the second scenario learned much more than how to handle mosquitoes. Approaching the lesson with a problem that all can relate to is an invitation to learn. Her students followed the entire expedition as they followed those insects. She also added relevancy by having her students create a Venn diagram comparing what Lewis and Clark took with them on this trip to what their own families would pack (Figure 1.6).

Making content relevant to our students' lives allows them to start making connections to prior knowledge immediately. Problem-based learning is experiential learning that is built around a real-world problem. Students engage in the process of identifying the problem and then finding a solution. This is an open-ended approach to learning the standards. Problems should touch on issues that professionals in the field of study would tackle in the real world (Wiggins & McTighe, 2005).

FIGURE 1.6	A Venn Diagram to Organize Students' Thinking About Similarities and Differences

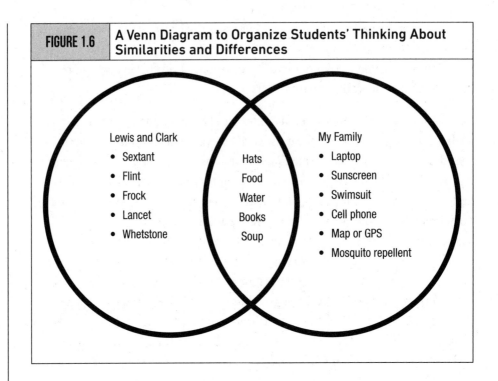

Lewis and Clark
- Sextant
- Flint
- Frock
- Lancet
- Whetstone

Hats
Food
Water
Books
Soup

My Family
- Laptop
- Sunscreen
- Swimsuit
- Cell phone
- Map or GPS
- Mosquito repellent

Relevancy, Relationships, and the Real World

Many of our diverse learners have difficulty relating to our goals and standards. Students from extreme poverty may be focusing on survival. Reading with fluency, understanding different forms of government, and knowing and applying concepts that explain how living things function, adapt, and change may not be the most crucial things to them. Nevertheless, it is our job to help students reach those benchmarks. The most powerful thing we can do is to help them find the relationship between their lives and our goals. It's not an easy task.

Here is an example using the Common Core State Standards:

ELA.SL.K.1a. Participate in collaborative conversations with diverse partners about kindergarten topics and texts with peers and adults in small and larger groups. (a) Follow agreed-upon rules for discussions (e.g., listening to others and taking turns speaking about the topics and texts under discussion). (b) Continue a conversation through multiple exchanges.

Kindergarten teacher Ms. Iwaszewicz of the Teaching Channel addresses this standard through a lesson in which students create and present posters on U.S. symbols. Using common symbols such as the U.S. flag, Statue of Liberty, bald eagle, the White House, and the Liberty Bell, she creates real-world connections for students. The students work collaboratively to make posters. Ms. Iwaszewicz continues the lesson with reciprocal teaching, a must-use strategy for brain-compatible classrooms. (See the video at www .teachingchannel.org/videos/teaching-facts-sfusd.)

 Mental Note: Our students remember what affects their lives.

A Novel Approach

Teachers have their own ways of reaching students, and often instinctively they know when it's time to try something new. Novelty is appealing to the brain. Perhaps you remember how the reticular activating system filters information. When the brain perceives incoming information to be unusual, it releases norepinephrine to focus attention; once the novelty is gone, this is no longer the case (Ratey, 2008).

Flooding the hippocampus with dopamine aids recall. To activate this "flashbulb memory" process, surprise students before or after introducing content you want them to remember. The retention of episodic memory is enhanced, in humans and animals, when something novel happens shortly before or after information is introduced (Takeuchi et al., 2016).

Here are a few ideas for adding novelty to your instruction:

• Begin with a bizarre fact that relates to your content. (Did you know that Abraham Lincoln wore bow ties?)

- Accessorize. (Wear a bow tie.)
- Hang something from the light or the overhead. (A bow tie?)
- Use a whistle or other sound your students are not accustomed to hearing.
- Play music pertaining to your content.
- Use a PowerPoint presentation with animation.

Presenting in Chunks

Research has suggested for years that teachers "chunk" information into small, easily understood portions (Marzano, 2017). New information is more easily received and placed into working memory this way simply because of the limits of working memory. In this way, students can focus on a bit of the information and reflect upon it before adding more. We can do this by having students read a few paragraphs of text and then stop to think and talk about it, or simply by verbally disseminating information. Just don't give your 5th graders all seven reasons for the westward expansion or all five steps in the story problem—feed them the information bit by bit.

Marzano (2017) suggests that we begin by using our pre-assessment data to plan our chunks of information. Creating a pre-assessment will provide you with information to help guide your entire unit. In fact, pre-assessment should be given at least a week before you are to begin a new unit. How well your students do will guide you as you prepare your lessons. It will also help you to differentiate your lessons, as you will probably have students who do well and others who need more help. If you pre-assess and all your students do well, you may be able to review some of the information in a larger chunk and add new material in smaller ones.

Some forms of pre-assessment include the following:

- Giving your post-assessment for the unit to see how well students do.
- Using a KWL or KWHLU chart (see Appendix B).
- Implementing the think-ink-pair-share strategy, which gives students the chance to write down what they know about the topic after a minute or two of thinking about it, then pairing up with another student and sharing ideas.

- Employing exit cards in the form of index cards handed out at the end of class and asking students either to free-write about what they know on a topic or supply the answer to a prompt (e.g., "Write three things you know about this topic, two things you might know, and one question you have").

☀ **Mental Note: "Assessment is today's means of modifying tomorrow's instruction."** —*Carol Ann Tomlinson*

From Sensory to Immediate Memory

We know through cognitive research that attention, motivation, relationships, relevance, learning preferences, and emotions are essential components of the "reaching" process. If we can get information from sensory memory into immediate memory, then we are on our way to long-term retention. As people mentally prepare for a task, they activate the prefrontal cortex, the area that performs higher-level functions and puts them in action. This advance preparation ensures that they will perform better than without prior activation (Kolb & Whishaw, 2009).

Reflection

1. Be aware of possible distractions in your classroom. For instance, auditory learners may be sensitive to sounds. If you can't have that noisy radiator fixed, try to seat the sound-sensitive student as far from the distraction as possible.
2. Think about extrinsic motivators that you may be using now. Some may be appropriate and necessary, but are others possibly undermining your students' innate desire to learn?
3. Discuss with colleagues ways to make your content more meaningful to your students. How can you explain the necessity of the content? Can you make it more desirable? Can you create interdisciplinary units that would be more relevant to your students?

4. Examine the climate of your classroom. Are you meeting the needs of your students? Are they comfortable with you and their peers? Could you change anything to make things better?

Reflect

Reflection is the stickiest of glues for the brain.

—*Patty McGee (2017)*

"This is a waste of my time!"

I looked up from my desk, where I had been writing in my reflection journal, quite surprised to realize that the voice was that of one of my more successful students. It was Patti, a good student who usually performed well enough for a B. I believed she could earn As, but there seemed to be a tiny disconnect between her receiving and retrieving systems. She almost always had that "aha" moment, and she was sometimes verbal about her feelings, as she was on this day.

"I only asked you to take a few minutes and write what you've learned and what you can do with it," I offered.

She looked at me, frustrated. "Yeah, but Mrs. Sprenger, I'm just getting into this unit, and I don't want to stop and think about this junk."

"Patti, trust me. I really believe that this task will make a difference in how well you remember what you're learning," I responded.

"So, we're supposed to stop our group discussions, get out our journals, and write a 'So What? Now What?' page. That's going to help? I didn't think I'd like to study anything about alternate forms of energy, and I'm enjoying it. This is like being interrupted in the middle of a TV show!"

At this point, several students stopped writing and nodded at her words. One spoke up.

"Patti's right. Aren't we wasting time?" he said.

"Listen. I'm trying this strategy because a professor of mine made me do it in a graduate class. It really helped my memory, and I think this type of strategy may add to what you remember. I believe it's worth a try, so do it, please," I requested.

I returned to my reflection journal and wrote "So What? Now What?" then added, "Maybe this wasn't a good idea. It really works for me, but maybe not for kids. Or am I just letting them instill doubts? The research says the brain needs time to reflect. I hope this works!"

A few weeks later, Patti entered my room sheepishly.

"Mrs. Sprenger? Look at this," she said. She handed me a graded test from another class, on which she'd received an A. The teacher had written on the page, "Patti, this is your best work. Your extended response answer shows that you have put some thought into your problem solving. Keep up the good work!"

"Congratulations!" I responded.

"Yeah, but I feel kinda bad about hassling you about our journals. You know that 'So What? Now What?' stuff?" she said, again looking embarrassed.

"Are you telling me that it worked?" I asked, surprised.

"I realized how much more I was remembering, Mrs. Sprenger. So I started using it in all my classes. Many of those Bs I always get are becoming As. I think I needed to think more about what I was learning. I just want you to know that some of that brain stuff you talk about really works!"

I smiled and thanked her. She moved on to her class. I opened my journal and began a new page. I wrote "So What? Now What?" and this time all I added was "Hooray!"

As this example shows, Reflection is not just the second step in the process of building memory; rather, it will be used throughout the entire process. It is wise to reflect after each step of memory building: after recoding, reinforcement, and each rehearsal. I tell my students that reflection is a form of rehearsal: They are ensuring their own memory success by using the reflection process.

I appreciate the following from *Learning and Leading with Habits of Mind* (2009, p. 223) by Costa and Kallick:

To be reflective means to mentally wander through where we have been and to try to make some sense out of it. Most classrooms are oriented more to the present and the future than to the past. Such an orientation means that students (and teachers) find it easier to discard what has happened and to move on without taking stock of the seemingly isolated experiences of the past.

☀ **Mental Note: Reflection is the first rehearsal.**

A Time to Be Silent and a Time to Speak

As in comedy, one secret of good teaching is timing. A response delivered too early or too late may not have the effect we expect. If a teacher responds too quickly, students don't learn as well (Stahl, 1994; Tobin, 1987). Now is the time to examine moments when our students need our silence. Silence that encourages reflective thinking can eventually lead to long-term memory.

The ability to reflect critically on one's experience and connect it to prior knowledge is essential to taking information from immediate memory and processing it in active working memory. Keep in mind that active working memory allows us to hold onto incoming information while our brains search long-term memory for patterns or connections that it recognizes. According to Williamson (1997), reflective practice may be a developmental learning process, and Wellington (1996) considers the possibility of different levels of attainment. Taking these views into consideration, teaching our students about the value of reflection may be a first step toward a *habit* of reflection.

It seems that our biggest enemy in education is time. We don't have enough time to cover the curriculum. We don't have enough time to prepare for the state test. We don't have time to give individual attention to our students. We barely have time to eat lunch, go to the restroom, and check our e-mail before classes begin again! When we are not doing two things at once, we must be wasting time. Still, some time is necessary for long-term retention to take hold. In this chapter, we will look specifically at *focus time, wait time,* and *time for reflection.*

☀ **Mental Note: Make time to take time.**

Focus Time

Imagine working busily at your computer. You may be writing a report for a class, an article for a journal, or a grant proposal. Suddenly, you can't focus your eyes very well, and you become "brain-dead"—you can't think of a single thing. Some have described this feeling as "hitting a wall." Your brain is tired, and it needs to rest. Perhaps you get up and find something else to do. You might rest for a few minutes, go to the refrigerator for a snack, or even shoot some baskets. After a few minutes, you feel better and can go back to your project.

Your students go through the same biological process. The difference, however, is that students must follow rules: no talking, no getting out of your seat, no snacking. They will give you subtle hints that they are losing interest at first; if you ignore these, they will grow into full-fledged disruptions.

A popular formula for determining student focus time is simply their age in minutes (see, e.g., DeFina, 2003). For example, on a good day, 10-year-olds should be able to focus for a good 10 minutes on any given stimulus. Any longer than that and students may start having private conversations, moving around the room, or looking for something else to do. This is perfectly natural. When the stimulation we are getting exceeds our capacity for concentration, the area of the brain expending energy on the task is running out of steam (or, in this case, glucose).

Perry (2016) suggests that neurons fatigue in four to eight minutes, regardless of student age. He suggests we begin our lessons by telling a story that taps into student emotions, followed by delivering facts (semantic information) and some conceptual understandings relevant to the original story. This strategy will keep the neural systems aroused without draining all of their energy.

> ☀ **Mental Note: Shifting the sensory stimulation you give students within their focus time will extend student attention.**

Wait Time

Slowing down may be a way of speeding up.

—*Mary Budd Rowe (1986)*

In the late 1960s, Mary Budd Rowe scrutinized instruction by teachers in a wide assortment of classroom settings. She established that teachers asked questions of students at the rate of two or three per minute. Only one second would pass before the questions were repeated or reshaped or before the teacher called on someone else. If students did respond quickly enough, the teacher then replied, on average, within 0.9 seconds by asking another question or responding to the given answer (Rowe, 1973).

For many of us, wait time is not a new idea, but it plays a vital role in the retention process. Offering students the opportunity to have just a few seconds to respond can give them enough reflective time to access prior knowledge, evaluate what has been said, and formulate an appropriate response.

According to Rowe, there are two wait-time intervals. The first is the time spent waiting for a question to be answered before the teacher changes the question, asks a more probing question, calls on another student, or answers the question himself. The second is the break after receiving a response and before saying anything. For the first interval, the average teacher waits 0.9 seconds, as previously mentioned; the wait for the second interval is usually even shorter. When these intervals are increased to at least three seconds, some remarkable changes occur (see Figure 2.1). Other more general effects are also noticeable: classroom discipline improves, teachers ask fewer and better questions (requiring higher-order thinking skills), and expectations for all students are raised (Rowe, 1986).

FIGURE 2.1	Impact of Wait Time as Determined by Rowe (1986)
• Responses change in length from a single word to whole statements.	
• Self-confidence increases.	
• Speculative thinking increases.	
• The questioning tone of the responses decreases.	
• Guessing, "I don't know," and inappropriate responses decrease.	
• Students "piggyback" on each other's ideas.	
• Responses by "slow" students increase.	
• The interaction becomes a student–student discussion, moderated by the teacher, instead of a teacher–student inquisition.	
• Students ask more questions.	
• Students propose more investigations.	
• *Student achievement improves.*	

Wait times are beneficial on the following occasions:

- Upon asking an initial question and prior to calling on a student or group of students for a response.
- Following the response from a student or group of students to the initial question.
- Subsequent to receiving a student's question and prior to responding.
- After asking a follow-up question.

Fogarty (2003) suggests two verbal responses to keep students thinking about an idea or concept. The first is "What else?" This question conveys to other students that there may be other acceptable answers and to keep trying. The other statement is "Tell me more." This request cues the students to do more in-depth thinking, dig for details, and synthesize information.

☀ **Mental Note: Students need time to answer and to question.**

Other Times to "Wait"

Stahl (1994) suggests other periods of silence that he calls "think time." Using the research of Rowe and others, he introduced the following think times:

- *Teacher pause time* is when the teacher is silent for three seconds or longer to consider what has taken place and how to proceed.
- *Impact pause time* is when the teacher pauses for several seconds (sometimes even minutes) until students notice and get back on task.
- *Within–student response pause time* is when a student pauses while giving an answer. Most teachers are uncomfortable with the pause and begin helping the student. Stahl suggests allowing at least three seconds here.
- *Post–student response wait time* is a silence of three seconds or longer given to allow other students to think about the response and respond to it.

Teacher pause time appears to be a luxury in our hectic schedules, but taking that time to consider or change the course of events in a lesson can be very helpful. Many of us do not use student pause time for two reasons. First, we don't want to embarrass the students, which we feel we are doing when we wait silently for an answer. Second, our students are so accustomed to what I call "video game" responses that we worry about keeping them all on task. Perhaps we are underestimating all of our students when we fall into these traps.

Here's an example of both student and teacher wait times in action:

During an 11th grade discussion on the topic of culture, I have asked Jonathon to answer the following question: "What are the cultural universals?" He begins to answer ("I think all cultures—") before pausing to think (within–student's response pause time). Perhaps I have caught him off guard, or maybe he's not accustomed to answering questions in this way. Some students start to snicker; others raise their hands to take over. I give those laughing a sharp look and turn my attention back to Jonathon.

He continues: "Yes, I definitely think all cultures have rules about what's right and what's wrong. Different ones, but they all have them."

Before I can write Jonathon's answer on the board, Jeffrey speaks.

"Every person has his own sense of right and wrong," he says. "Let's find out what each person in this class considers acceptable."

I hesitate. I need time to decide whether I want to open this can of worms (teacher pause time). Do I want to take this idea and run with it? Are my students comfortable enough with each other and with me to open up? The students appear excited about it.

"OK," I begin. "Everyone make your own list of what you think is unacceptable behavior."

Hurry Up and Wait

In the beginning, wait time may feel awkward to you and your students. Keep in mind that lower-level questions require less wait time, and higher-level questions may take 5 to 10 minutes. In the latter case, expect all students to be pondering the question. Acknowledge students who are ready with an answer, but do not interrupt the waiting period. Give your students those seconds they need. The silence may be uncomfortable, so count or check the second hand on your watch as you wait for time to pass. Better yet, count the number of "aha!" looks on your students' faces. When you accept responses, refrain from commenting on answers. A simple "thank you" acknowledges a contribution without giving verbal rewards.

Imagine yourself searching long-term memory for a name, a book title, or a phone number. You are scanning all sorts of information tucked neatly away in your brain. Now imagine being interrupted by someone talking while you are searching. Worse yet, imagine someone interrupting your thoughts with an answer you were trying to find yourself. Frustrating, huh?

That's why wait time is so important. Some of us need a bit more time than others to access information.

☀ **Mental Note: Wait time allows students to search their long-term memory while holding onto new information.**

Time for Reflection

Studies examining how the brain works during reflection using MRI or PET scans show that reflection is processed in the frontal lobes of the brain (Johnson et al., 2002), sometimes referred to as the executive area of the brain. Working memory is also processed here. Note that reflection time is not the same as *downtime,* which refers to the time of day when the brain is less likely to take in information (Erlauer, 2003). Rather, reflection takes place in lessons and units throughout the school day.

Atkins and Murphy (1993) have identified three stages in the reflective process—an awareness of uncomfortable feelings, followed first by a critical analysis of the situation and then by the development of a new perspective on it. Burrows (1995) defines the process of reflecting as an "exploration and discovery to make sense of new information and leads on to a process of critical reflection, reframing problems and identifying probable consequences" (p. 346). Kemmis's (1985) description of the process differs. He views the reflective process as analytical, focusing inward on one's own thoughts and processes and focusing outward on the situation at hand. From the learner's perspective, Boud, Keough, and Walker (1985) say that reflection is a combination of intellectual and affective activities in which students engage to explore their experiences, leading them to a new understanding. According to Dewey (1910/1997), "Reflection—thought in its best sense . . . is turning a topic over in various aspects and in various lights so that nothing significant about it shall be overlooked—almost as one might turn a stone over to see what its hidden side is like or what is covered by it" (p. 57).

I like to explain reflection to my students as a chance for them not only to connect new knowledge to what they already know but also to question the source—whether that source is myself, the author of their text, or anything else. I ask them to be detectives getting to the heart of the matter, and I suggest that *their* hearts—their feelings and opinions—are important to the process.

Perkins (1995) refers to three intelligences: *neural intelligence, experiential intelligence,* and *reflective intelligence.* Neural intelligence refers to how well the brain makes and keeps connections. Experiential intelligence encompasses the personal experiences we have that contribute to intelligent behavior. Reflective intelligence comprises knowledge, understanding, and attitudes about how our minds should be used. Perkins states that the second two, experiential and reflective, are learnable intelligences, and he considers reflective intelligence as the control system for the other intelligences.

The consensus is that reflection can and must be taught. To that end, what are some good reflective practices? Dickman and Blair (2002) suggest that "the reflective nature of intelligence can be interpreted as the conscious bending back of information patterns to discern potential relationships of peril or promise" (p. 96). They add that a reflection task requires five areas:

1. *Physiological:* Your brain literally lights up with activity as you reflect. The more novel the item of reflection, the more activity is present.
2. *Social:* Reflection promotes social experience as the brain seeks out other brains. As you reflect, finding others to collaborate with or corroborate your thoughts is common.
3. *Emotional:* Evaluation is part of the reflective process. To value something worth your reflection, emotion must be involved.
4. *Constructive:* Knowledge is constructed during the reflective process. New patterns of thinking may be assembled and old patterns retrieved.
5. *Dispositional:* From these new patterns, habits may be formed.

☀ **Mental Note: Reflection is a learned habit.**

The Growth Mindset

Reflection will be easier and more worthwhile if your students believe that they can learn and achieve through hard work. They need to believe that neither intelligence nor past experiences will prevent them from learning. It doesn't matter that they didn't do well last year; they can change the pattern through effort and trial and error.

Students who are in the present and focused on the future—what Carol Dweck (2006) calls a *growth mindset*—have the opportunity to reflect on their learning and make connections to prior knowledge. By contrast, students who focus more on the past than the future and believe that their level of achievement is bred in the bone have a *fixed mindset*. We all need to have a growth mindset, and this can be taught. Dweck offers the following four steps for changing a fixed mindset:

1. *Learn to hear your fixed-mindset voice.* It may be telling you that you cannot do something.
2. *Recognize that you have a choice.* You can either listen to that fixed voice and give up on getting better, or ignore it and start improving.
3. *Answer your fixed mindset with a growth mindset.* If your fixed-mindset voice tells you that you cannot do something, tell it that even if you cannot do it the first time, lots of people fail and try again. You are one of those people!
4. *Take control of the voices.* Take action! Know that every challenge may require hard work and some changes, but you can do it!

Modeling these four steps in the classroom will make a difference for your students. Talk aloud as you tackle new challenges: "I am having trouble with the whiteboard today. The power supply doesn't seem to be working. I have to figure out how to fix this. I am not very good with mechanical things, but I am going to have to learn to read the flowchart that comes with the whiteboard manual. Let me see if I can understand this. There is a light blinking. I need to find which light it is and find the light on the chart. I will figure this out. While I am doing this, turn to your neighbor and discuss the math problem that is on the bulletin board. I know you'll have fun with it!" You have a problem. You don't know how to fix it. But you will figure it out!

As students begin to change their mindsets, the reflection process will allow them to see more possibilities for the material they are reflecting upon and for themselves.

The Seven Habits of Highly Reflective Classrooms

OK, so I borrowed a catchy phrase from Stephen Covey's *The Seven Habits of Highly Effective People* (1989). When used purposefully and often, these reflective strategies can become habits for you and your students. According to Costa and Kallick (2000), thinking about our thinking is itself one of the 16 habits of mind. "Intelligent people," they say, "plan for, reflect on, and evaluate the quality of their own thinking skills and strategies" (p. 5).

We want our students to be aware of their skills, strategies, and experiences. In *Educating Minds and Hearts*, Cohen (1999) suggests "that self-reflective capacities on the one hand and the ability to recognize what others are thinking and feeling on the other provide the foundation for children to understand, manage, and express the social and emotional aspects of life" (p. 11).

 Mental Note: "Reflection fosters a disposition toward discovery and connection-making." —*Jennifer Fletcher*

Habit 1: Questioning

Questioning is at the heart of reflection. Robert Marzano identifies four types of questions: *detail*, *category*, *elaborating*, and *evidence* (Marzano Center, 2015). Johnson (1995) categorizes questions as follows: *quantity, compare/contrast, feelings/opinions/point of view/personification, "What if,"* and *"How come?"* She then further categorizes questions as either *active* (those that students ask) or *passive* (those that students answer). In the reflective process, we want students to engage with both types by asking themselves questions and searching for the answers. Teachers must model this type of questioning for it to become a habit among students. Fogarty (2003) refers to *fat* and *skinny* questions. Fat questions require discussion and explanation with examples, whereas *skinny* questions require simple yes/no responses. McTighe and Wiggins (2013) discuss the concept of *essential* questions. These questions are meant to refine and organize the curriculum in the classroom.

Reflective questions often start with *why* or *how*. When you offer your students these questions, you are inviting them to ask themselves, "How do I know what I know?" Asking factual questions such as "Who?" "When?" or "Where?" will not lead them to the connections they can discover through more thought-provoking, higher-level questions.

Choose a questioning technique and get into the habit of using it. When you begin with the end in mind, you must devise several essential questions for your unit. Ask students one of these questions as you introduce material, and then offer it to them again for their reflection. Do this often enough, and students will begin to ask themselves extension questions. Then the habit will be set!

Peter Pappas (2010) has created the following "reflection taxonomy" based on Bloom's Taxonomy:

- Remembering: What did I do?
- Understanding: What was important about it?
- Applying: Where could I use this again?
- Analyzing: Do I see any patterns in what I did?
- Evaluating: How well did I do?
- Creating: What should I do next?

I would personally tweak two of these questions to add a dimension of relevance: *Understanding: How was this important to me?* and *Analyzing: How is this similar to anything else that I know?*

Rothstein and Santana (2011) offer a plan for getting students to start asking questions. Their Question Formulation Technique involves the following six steps:

1. Design a question focus.
2. Produce questions.

3. Work with closed-ended and open-ended questions.

4. Prioritize questions.

5. Plan next steps.

6. Reflect.

In discussing her framework for teaching, Charlotte Danielson (2011) emphasizes the importance of questioning in the classroom: "Questioning and discussion are the only instructional strategies specifically referred to in the Framework for Teaching, a decision that reflects their central importance to teachers' practice" (p. 51). Other evaluation frameworks also consider student questioning a sign of exceptional teaching.

Mental Note: "The important thing is not to stop questioning." —*Albert Einstein*

Mental Note: "Teachers who promote reflective classrooms ensure that students are fully engaged in the process of making meaning."—*Arthur L. Costa and Bena Kallick (2009)*

Habit 2: Visualizing

A picture is worth a thousand words, or so the saying goes. Students who can visualize can temporarily store a lot of information in that relatively small space known as working memory. According to Howard Gardner's (1983) theory of multiple intelligences, most people possess a visual/spatial intelligence. The ability to make use of this intelligence while receiving information in other forms affords the possibility of multiple coding, which is an area that needs to be strengthened in all students. PET scans show that visual information causes a great deal of brain activity in the right hemisphere (Burmark, 2002).

Expecting your students to be able to visualize regardless of their learning preferences may seem like an intrusion, but I have seen all kinds of learners use mind maps successfully to retrieve information. For young students, it is beneficial to ask that they draw what they are visualizing.

We all have visual schemas or mental maps that we use on a regular basis (Armstrong, 1993). These episodic memory maps get us where we are going. Reminders of role models who use similar strategies may encourage your students to try them. For example, many of the sports fans in my classes knew that professional athletes use visualization techniques. Kerri Walsh and Misty May Treanor, the most successful female beach volleyball team in history, use visualization as part of their training routine (Williams, 2015).

Albert Einstein, Charles Darwin, and Sigmund Freud also used visual thinking, employing images to conjure up their theories. For example, Einstein pictured what it would be like to ride on a beam of light to visualize his theory of relativity.

Get your students started on visualization by having them put down on paper some of the following visual maps that they might already have stored in their memories:

- Draw a map from home to school.
- A map of the United States.
- An abstract concept, such as freedom.
- A blueprint of the school or your classroom.

Once students realize that they have these mental pictures in their heads, encourage them to habitually use their visualization powers to reflect on new information.

Habit 3: Journaling

Seven thousand notebook pages belonging to Leonardo da Vinci still exist. He always carried a notebook with him. He wrote down everything, including daily observations, jokes, and plans for new inventions (Gelb, 1998). Have your students keep a journal, too. Reflection time can involve writing questions, observations, connections to prior knowledge, or any insights into the lesson presented. If you have reached your students, they will have something to record in their journals. Writing about an experience provides students with a sense of control (Restak, 2000). Supplying reflection stems such as the following may be helpful in the beginning:

- I learned . . .
- I want to learn more about . . .
- I liked . . .
- I did not like . . .
- I did not understand . . .
- I would have liked (or understood) it better if . . .

Habit 4: Using Thinking Directives

Give your students time to think about the information they have received. Here are a few thinking directives you might use, though I encourage you to come up with your own creative ones:

- Think about . . .
- Think back to a time when . . .
- Imagine a future when . . .
- Put yourself in someone else's shoes. What would they think about . . .
- Think reproductively: How has this happened before?
- Think productively: How many ways can I approach this?
- Think of a comparison, analogy, or metaphor.

Habit 5: Thinking Like a PMI Chart

A PMI chart is a graphic organizer that offers students an organized reflection time. The *P* stands for *plus*: What part of what we just covered is positive for you? The *M* stands for *minus*: Are there topics or concepts that you don't like or understand? The *I* represents *interesting*: What parts of this lesson do you find interesting?

A PMI chart can be set up horizontally or vertically. If your students use this chart several times, they may then be able to think using the categories. You may also substitute *implications* for *interesting*, which may be a good alternative for older students. (See Appendix B for examples of this and other graphic organizers.)

Habit 6: Collaboration

Students must first have developed collaborative skills for this habit to be successful. If you have taught emotional intelligence skills as an avenue for reaching your students as discussed in Chapter 1, then your students should be able to handle the task of reflecting with others.

At the 2004 ASCD Annual Conference, I had the pleasure of hearing Margaret Wheatley speak on the topic of her recent book, *Turning to One Another: Simple Conversations to Restore Hope to the Future*. She discussed how, in our present society, we are trying to get humans to work at the same speed as machines. "We are losing our time to think," she said. "We are losing our time to be together." She suggested that we reclaim the time we need to reflect, listen, and understand each other. Collaborating during the reflective step gives our students the opportunity to do this.

Johnson, Johnson, and Holubec (2007) have identified the following five essential elements of effective cooperative learning. Students must

1. Agree that they are "in this together,"
2. Help each other learn and celebrate successes,
3. Take responsibility for contributions,
4. Build group skills such as conflict resolution, and
5. Reflect on group and individual processing.

Johnson and colleagues (2007) encourage teachers to monitor student collaboration. Tileston (2000) suggests doing this through "cruise control": "cruising" through the room to keep students on task. This is also the first opportunity to check for understanding. As the students share their reflections, you may be able to catch misconceptions. Interrupting the collaboration may be an option, or you may take time after the reflective collaboration to make some clarifications.

Figure 2.2. cites a procedure for reflective collaboration; Figure 2.3 presents a rubric for collaboration.

FIGURE 2.2	Collaboration Procedure

1. Model what this type of collaboration could entail.

2. Discuss the social skills necessary, and practice those.

3. Begin with pairs. You may want to do a think-pair-share. Be sure the students have a few moments to think before they join their partner.

4. Decide how the partners will be picked. I always suggest that you do the choosing, not the students. Think about the possibilities: random pairs, homogeneous pairs, gender pairs, and so forth.

5. Keep track of time. Some students will have a greater grasp of the material than others.

6. Provide for some accountability, but keep it light, as this is a personal reflection.

FIGURE 2.3	Sample Rubric for Reflective Collaboration				
	Beginning 1	Developing 2	Accomplished 3	Excellent 4	Score
Contributing					
Shares Information	Does not relay any information to teammates	Relays very little information— some relates to the topic	Relays some basic information— most relates to the topic	Relays much information— all relates to the topic	
Valuing Others' Perspectives					
Listens	Always talking—no one else gets a chance	Does most of the talking— rarely gives others a chance	Sometimes listens, but still talks a lot	Listens and speaks equally	
Cooperation	Usually argues with teammates	Sometimes argues	Rarely argues	Never argues with teammates	
				Total	

Habit 7: Four-Corner Reflection

This multimodal approach to reflecting may incorporate movement, music, discussion, and visuals. Here's how it works:

1. Place a chart listing key ideas in each corner of the room.
2. Have students gather in groups in each corner to discuss the ideas and add their thoughts and any new ideas to the chart.
3. After five minutes, play music or blow a whistle to signal that it is time for students to rotate to the next corner.
4. Students repeat the process for each corner.
5. The last group at each corner is responsible for summarizing the information on the chart.
6. Engage in whole-group discussion.

As you get into the habit of offering students reflection time, you may need to become selective. Your content may dictate which reflective habit you choose. For instance, consider an interdisciplinary unit on the Holocaust. Such a sensitive topic may not lend itself well to open discussion and may be better served through reflective journaling. By contrast, a science unit on the weather would be perfect for a four-corner reflection, with different weather conditions displayed at each corner.

Mental Note: As adults, we reflect as we learn. Organizing the reflection through one of the seven habits helps young people make connections with prior knowledge, as they mentally arrange what they have received.

Teacher Reflection

It is important that teachers receive or provide themselves with reflection time. Senge and colleagues (2000) propose that there are three different components of reflection:

1. *Reconsidering:* Question yourself. Are you getting your points across? Are your expectations where they should be? Challenge your assumptions and conclusions.
2. *Reconnecting:* Who else has attempted this in a different way? Look at trends, data, and methods of implementation.
3. *Reframing:* Do some scenario planning, incorporating diverse possibilities. Imagine yourself and your students in each scenario.

Stronge (2007) notes that reflection is integral to professionalism. Research shows that effective teachers may reflect formally or informally, that students with high achievement rates have teachers who use reflection on their work as an important component for improvement, and that teachers who reflect maintain high expectations for students.

....

Mental Note: Teachers who use and model reflective practice will have a better understanding of and higher expectations for their students' reflective capabilities.

....

Reflection as Assessment

Reflections can serve as informal assessments. When you are on cruise control, gather as much information as you can. Your students' reflections will offer you the information you need to determine whether they are ready for the next step in the process: recoding. You may want to determine whether they can make connections by using an assessment rubric for the seven habits (see Figure 2.4).

Reflection in Action

I was wearing my Minnie Mouse costume, and the students chuckled as they entered the room. I had a stuffed Mickey Mouse and Donald Duck on the overhead table. As I explained the process for writing a reflection essay as a group, we compared and contrasted Mickey and Donald. This was a simple task for my students,

FIGURE 2.4	Assessment Rubric for Reflection. Students scoring a 3 or 4 are ready for step 3, Recoding				
Reflective Habit	**1**	**2**	**3**	**4**	**Score**
	The student has	The student has	The student has	The student has	
Questioning	No questions answered or generated	Questions generated are unrelated; questions answered don't relate	One related question	Several related questions	
Visualizing	No picture	Unrelated picture	A drawing	Ability to describe her mental picture	
Journaling	Little or no writing	Unrelated writing	Repetition of what was said	Connections between prior knowledge and new information	
Thinking Directives	No directives	Unrelated thoughts	Followed directive	Followed directive and goes beyond	
PMI	No chart	Incomplete information	Completed chart	Completed mental chart	
Collaboration	No participation	Little participation	Short discussion	Obvious understanding through discussion	
Four Corner	No interaction or notes	Little interaction; few notes	Some interaction; some notes	Obvious understanding through interaction and notes	

and that's how I wanted it: I wanted their working memories to concentrate on the form of writing. The emotion and novelty helped me reach my students. It was a short piece, so I was able to keep them attentive throughout. I wrote the similarities in red marker and the differences in green. The colors seemed to intrigue some of the students.

Now it was time for reflection. I called on the habit of visualizing. "I want you to visualize two other characters that you can compare and contrast using only physical characteristics," I said. "Picture them in your mind, and make a mental list of what those similarities and differences are." I gave the students five minutes for reflection. Most of them seemed to be making connections. Some nodded, some laughed. Others looked very serious. A few students seemed confused.

"Let's reflect a little more and get a concrete look at this," I said. "Take a sheet of paper and draw your characters. As you compare physical characteristics, draw arrows to them."

All the students immediately got to work. Students who had not seemed able to reflect visually or to understand the lesson earlier began to apply what they had learned. I cruised the room and determined whether we needed to create another group essay or they were ready to write their own.

 Mental Note: The process of reflecting can be affected by learning preference, emotional states, or specific content. Be prepared to kick one habit for another.

Thinking About Information in Working Memory

After reviewing studies on teaching strategies to developmentally disabled learners, Belmont, Butterfield, and Ferretti (cited in Perkins, 1995) concluded that these students would transfer memory strategies to other settings and circumstances *if they were taught self-monitoring strategies along with the memory strategies.* The self-monitoring strategy they were taught was questioning.

Thinking about our thinking is a necessary skill for lifelong learning. Reflective habits lead us to a better understanding of how our brains work. Students need to have the ability and skills to plan, monitor, and evaluate their thinking. This leads to controlling thinking and behavior. Knowing how and why we think the way we do is *metacognition*, which leads to applying thinking skills in new situations.

Thus far in our discussion, students have been reached through sensory and immediate memory and are now manipulating the facts and concepts in working memory. As they strive to make connections, they are rehearsing the new learning and finding ways to attach it to prior knowledge.

Reflection

1. Some students respond better to concrete reflection; that is, they need to "do it" in order to "see it." Be ready to shift gears when a reflection piece isn't working for everyone.
2. With the emphasis in most schools on coverage and testing, reflection seems like an extravagance. Keep in mind that this is the step that can make the difference in reaching accessible memories. It marks the beginning of ownership of the information.
3. Some students may over-reflect on and overanalyze certain material or situations, which is why time limits are important for these sessions. Others may not have a handle on the material and be unable to do much reflection. Too much time allows these students to disrupt others.
4. Whichever practice you use for your students' reflection, keep in mind that you are allowing their brains time to make important associations.

Recode

You don't know anything clearly unless you can state it in writing.

—*S. I. Hayakawa*

*It was the week before the start of the new school year, and I was having a movie marathon, watching films that inspire me to embrace my profession—*Mr. Holland's Opus, Stand and Deliver, Dead Poets Society, Dangerous Minds. *There is a scene in* Dangerous Minds *where LouAnne Johnson, the teacher in the movie, introduces poetry to her kids and says, "It's written in code. You have to break the code." As I watched it, it suddenly dawned on me that I was neglecting to make this point to my students.*

Our students are constantly trying to break a code—a textbook code, a lecture code, a video code, a website code. Language varies from medium to medium, and students' understanding of language varies depending on their backgrounds. I feel as though I have discovered a memory fixative: If my students can "break the code" and recode the information in their own language, not only will they have a better understanding of it, but they will also have a better memory of it.

What Is Recoding?

Recoding is the ability to take information from different sources and generate it in your own language. It can be symbolic, as in drawing pictures or constructing through movement—though when students are tested, they must have the ability to share information linguistically. At some point in the seven-step process of teaching students to remember, therefore, information must be manipulated through paper and pencil.

According to Levine (2002), some students who have trouble recoding are experiencing short-term memory problems. He defines *recoding* as the ability to summarize and paraphrase. Levine suggests that we encourage students to use their strongest sensory pathway in order to work with this problem.

I agree with S. I. Hayakawa's quote at the beginning of this chapter. If students can write about what they know, then we know that they know it. They are using their ability to recall information. So, for assessment purposes, an essay or other form of authentic assessment provides us with more information than a multiple-choice test. During the recoding step, we want students to be able to write down what they understand thus far about what they're learning. At first, some students may have trouble with writing and need to use a different mode of expression. This calls for differentiation—meeting learners where they are and offering them appropriate and challenging options to achieve success (Tomlinson, 2014). If we are truly differentiating our classrooms, then we should permit some choice in the recoding process. After the students can show their understanding, it is time for them to stretch to another medium (Sprenger, 2003). Because our instruction is covering standards that will be assessed on a paper-and-pencil test, it is paramount that we encourage students to work on using their semantic pathways.

☀ **Mental Note: Self-generated material is better remembered.**

Why Recode?

I was delivering a presentation on memory to about 1,400 people. "Stand up if you have something good to say about your memory," I began. A dozen people stood up.

"Raise your hand if you lose your keys," I said next. All hands were raised.

"How many of you have a specific spot in your home or office where you always put your keys?" Again, all hands. "Except when you don't!" Laughter and nodding.

"Believe me, I have been tempted to call the psychic hotline more than once to find out where those darn keys are," I told the audience. "Memory research will make us all feel better. You see, you can't retrieve information that you haven't stored. When your keys aren't where they are supposed to be, it's because you have so many things on your mind that you didn't pay attention to where you put them. You didn't use the typical organizational model that you usually do. That's why tracing your steps will often work."

Most memory experts (e.g., Small, 2003) suggest that organization is the key to a good memory. Systematically arranging information according to groups, patterns, and other structures can make the difference between success and failure in the storage and retrieval of information.

In my seminars, I will often read a list of about 10 words and have participants wait a few seconds before writing them down. Most people are usually unable to write down every word at first; however, when I tell them a *category* that the words might fit in, they are often able to retrieve them (see Figure 3.1 for an example of this technique). I then like to emphasize to the group how important it is for them to show their students ways to organize information.

According to Engle, Kane, and Tuholski (1999), people with higher working memory capacity do better than their peers on standardized college admission tests, intelligence tests, and reading comprehension tests. Research from the Social Cognitive Laboratory at North Carolina State University strongly suggests that writing can affect working memory capacity in general. The study used three groups: One group wrote about a positive experience, one wrote about a negative experience, and one wrote about daily activities. Working memory improved in all three groups (Klein & Boals, 2001).

Other research supports the effectiveness of self-generated material. Bruning, Schraw, and Ronning (1999) demonstrated that when students generate their own context for meaning, memory improves. An example of the

FIGURE 3.1	Organizing by Category to Remember 20 Words

Apple	Car
Hammer	Pear
Train	Rose
Orange	Wrench
Lily	Squirrel
Daisy	Airplane
Zebra	Lion
Tulip	Pliers
Saw	Camel
Cherry	Boat

Fruit	Animals	Flowers	Transportation	Tools
Apple	Squirrel	Rose	Car	Hammer
Pear	Camel	Lily	Train	Wrench
Orange	Zebra	Tulip	Airplane	Pliers
Cherry	Lion	Daisy	Boat	Saw

application of this research is found in current curriculum design for vocabulary. It is important that students generate their own definition or description of a word, as doing so makes the word and its definition personally relevant (Tileston, 2011). Research on the generation effect consistently shows that students do better when they make their own meaning (Rabinowitz & Craik, 1986).

Self-generation makes sense, because students create their own understanding, which involves taking explicit, semantic material and coding it in a personal way. This adds some implicit memory to the memory-making process. When true understanding takes place, emotions are involved. The process of recoding in some cases will involve movement and perhaps a procedural component, both of which strengthen the possibility of long-term retention.

Organization is significant in the recoding process of factual information. Our brains will organize information, but if we are not in control of that organization, we may have difficulty accessing the relevant memory. Recoding offers students the opportunity to organize thoughts, facts, and concepts in a way that is compatible not only with the way their brains think but also with the specific type of material.

When information will be accessed in the same way repeatedly and does not require learning a related concept, the organization process may be quite different. For instance, we learn the multiplication tables and are expected to retrieve them automatically and in the same way every time. Although we learn them in a rote fashion, understanding the concepts behind the learning is essential.

Organization can be a problem for some students, who may have trouble finding the materials they need, managing their time to get things done, managing complex tasks, prioritizing, or organizing their thoughts (Levine, 2003). The recoding experience will offer them strategies, sometimes called *mental models* or *schemata*, that will be useful in many situations.

Note Taking Versus Note Making

Teachers sometimes ask if students are recoding when they take notes during a lecture. If you have a brain-compatible classroom, you actually don't want students taking notes while they are listening to you (Jensen & Nickelson, 2008). We know from the research that the brain cannot multitask. Taking notes while trying to take in information is a distraction that forces the brain to task-switch (Medina, 2014). Also, the recoding required in the seven steps takes place only after reflection. Students generally do not have time to reflect while they are using the note-taking process. It is far better to have students skip the note taking under these circumstances and simply listen for understanding. If you stop lecturing every few minutes and allow students to write things down, they are far more likely to absorb the information.

In essence, recoding would be the process of note *making*—writing things down in one's own words without interruption and even adding some prior knowledge or new connections to the material.

Mental Note: Asking students to retrieve information right after it has been introduced promotes retention (e.g., "Tell a neighbor what you just learned!").

Factual, Conceptual, and Procedural Knowledge

Information that has been received and reflected upon is developed for recoding. This may include factual knowledge, conceptual knowledge, or procedural knowledge. According to Anderson and colleagues (2001),

- Recoding falls into the *cognitive process* category of understanding for conceptual knowledge—constructing meaning from instructional messages, including oral, written, and graphic communication.
- Procedural knowledge is in the *process category*—applying, carrying out, or using a procedure in a given situation.
- Factual knowledge falls under the *remember* category: Recoding allows us to assess the perceptions and comprehension our students have of the content being covered. In some instances, the significance of the content to the student may also be derived from this practice.

Recoding Factual Knowledge

Factual knowledge includes terminology and details. This is information that needs to be remembered in much the same form that it is taught. Knowing this information may be an important basis for conceptual and procedural learning. According to Sternberg, Grigorenko, and Jarvin (2001), "One cannot analyze what one knows (analytical thinking), go beyond what one knows (creative thinking), or apply what one knows (practical thinking) if one does not know anything" (p. 48).

Recoding factual information may entail different processes for different students. For some, writing the information several times may help, as in learning spelling words. Others may find oral repetition more effective. Still others may prefer to create symbols, songs, or movements.

We can examine vocabulary as one type of factual knowledge. Research demonstrates that vocabulary words need to be taught through direct instruction. In order for our students to better understand words in context, they need to be introduced in advance. The research also suggests that associating an image with a word is the best way to learn it (Marzano, Pickering, & Pollack, 2001). Here are suggested steps for teaching vocabulary:

1. Choose words that are critical to the content.
2. Introduce those words and their meanings with an image to represent each one.
3. Let students reflect on the meanings and images.
4. Ask students to create an image themselves to associate with each word.

Mental Note: Factual information is the basis for conceptual understanding.

Recoding Conceptual Knowledge

Anderson and colleagues (2001) note that seven cognitive processes help the brain construct meaning from instructional messages: *interpreting, exemplifying, classifying, summarizing, inferring, comparing,* and *explaining.* These processes allow students not only to remember but also to transfer information and eventually use it in unanticipated situations.

Interpreting. In the clearest sense of the word, *recoding* is interpreting, or changing information from one form into another. Whenever our students take notes when we speak, they are interpreting our words, unless they are writing what we say verbatim. Subcategories of interpreting include *paraphrasing, clarifying,* and *translating.* Paraphrasing, one of the most used subcategories, involves putting a passage from a source into one's own words while retaining the original meaning and crediting the original source. During the recoding process, students may think of themselves as paraphrasing what you have presented to them.

The following paraphrasing strategy is part of the Whole Brain Teaching approach designed by Chris Biffle (2013). Following a teacher lecture, students break into pairs and share what they have learned in their own words, perhaps taking notes as well. Students are now part of the teaching that is going on, and they are delivering content to one another in a multisensory way. Students learn the most about any content when they are the ones who get to teach it. An additional benefit of this technique is that, unlike most traditional instruments, the teacher can tell at a glance if every student is engaged in the lesson or not.

Many students will gain from direct instruction in interpreting (Olivier & Bowler, 1996). Interpretations may take many forms: Students could paraphrase a famous speech, draw an illustration of the process of mitosis, write a mathematical equation from a story problem, or create a dance to translate the feelings of the Pilgrims or the Indians. We want to prepare our students to apply their interpretations in other situations, as will be expected of them in the real world and on standardized tests. Stiggins (2004) suggests offering interpretive exercises for assessment that ask students to paraphrase the contents of a brief passage, table, or chart.

Exemplifying. Finding examples of learning material in the world around them is a task that many students enjoy. For example, a common assignment in geometry is to have students walk through their school in search of different types of angles.

A very popular graphic organizer for exemplifying was created by Dorothy Frayer and her colleagues at the University of Wisconsin. Originally designed as a vocabulary graphic organizer, it is often used for any concept at all grade levels and content areas. The original organizer has four quadrants with the following headings: *description, characteristics or facts, examples,* and *nonexamples.* The word or concept being examined is placed in the middle. (See Figure B.11 in Appendix B for an example.) This organizer encourages higher-order thinking and accessing background knowledge and is useful for individuals, small groups, and large groups.

According to Kahn (2002), a good set of examples will include simple examples, typical examples, and unusual examples, and will be complemented by some nonexamples. While *simple* examples are self-explanatory, *typical* examples contain all of the characteristics of the idea with nothing left out. *Unusual* examples indicate that the student can "step outside the box" and really understands the material. *Nonexamples* clarify understanding; when a student knows what does not qualify as an example, she has a better idea of the concept.

Storytelling can be part of exemplifying. Students love to tell stories, and stories can include patterns that represent the important components of the principle or concept. According to Damasio (1999), telling stories "is probably a brain obsession and probably begins relatively early both in terms of evolution and in terms of the complexity. Telling stories precedes language, since it is, in fact, a condition for language, and it is based not just in the cerebral cortex but elsewhere in the brain and in the right hemisphere as well as the left" (p. 189). Allen and Scozzi (2012) state that stories create a structure in which ideas connect and assist in critical thinking. Caine and Caine (1994) note, "There is strong reason to believe that organization of information in story form is a natural brain process" (p. 122). Why fight Mother Nature? If it works with your content, encourage your students to recode using stories.

Illustrations are another way to exemplify. Burmark (2002) cites a study showing that groups using illustrated texts perform 36 percent better at recall than groups using text alone. Creating or finding illustrations to exemplify conceptual understanding may be especially important and helpful to visual and kinesthetic learners.

Classifying. The ability to conceive that something fits into a particular category requires us to understand its distinguishing features. According to Anderson and colleagues (2001), classifying and exemplifying are complementary abilities. To exemplify, we begin with a general concept or principle and narrow down to specific examples; to classify, we do the exact opposite. Classification tasks may be teacher directed or student directed (Dean, Hubbell, Pitler, & Stone, 2012). In *teacher-directed* tasks, students are given the elements to classify, as well as the categories for classification ("Make a list of the Civil War heroes we just discussed. Create categories of your choosing, but make sure they relate to one of our goals, such as 'Students will understand key people involved in the Civil War.'"). When they recode the information, they determine under which category each element falls and focus on figuring out why. In *student-directed* classification tasks, students must take elements and create the categories themselves ("Make a list of the Civil War heroes we just discussed. Use the following categories to show that you understand the key people involved in the war: Affiliation, Position, and Battles Fought.")

The student-directed classification requires higher cognitive processes, so it is quite possible to differentiate using this strategy. Give students who are ready for higher-level processes a student-directed classification project and students who are not at the same readiness level a teacher-directed project. Graphic organizers such as T-charts, mind maps, webs, and Venn diagrams can all be helpful for classifying (see Appendix B). Classifying is included in the research on identifying similarities and differences, which shows that the percentile gain in learning for students who receive lessons on similarities and differences is between 31 and 46 percent (Dean, Hubbell, Pitler, & Stone, 2012).

Are some categories better than others? Absolutely. Consider a common problem: labeling files in your computer. Have you ever completed a file and thought of different names for it? At the time you name the file, you have plenty of information about the topic in your working memory—so much that you are certain that you will have no problem finding the file with the clever title you have chosen. Later, when it is time to access the file, you search and search, but the name you used does not trigger any memories. You may have to check several files before you find what you need. Our brains are much the same as our computers. If the categories and classifications are not strong and explanatory, we may have difficulty storing and retrieving the information (Baddeley, 1999).

Summarizing. This recoding strategy involves constructing a representation of information; using it has been shown to result in student percentile gains of up to 47 percent (Marzano, Pickering, & Pollack, 2001). There are two fundamentals of summarizing: filling in missing parts and translating information into an amalgamated form (Marzano, Pickering, & Pollack, 2001). Summarizing includes extracting themes and main ideas, a skill that is often assessed on standardized achievement tests. According to Levine (2002), "All kids need to strengthen their summarization skills" (p. 148).

If students can read one or more articles and create a summary of important concepts or ideas, they can use this skill in a variety of settings. It is important that students understand that they need to do the following to summarize:

- Take out information that is not important.
- Delete repetitive information.
- Combine single elements into one category (e.g., *gold, silver,* and *nickel* become *metals*).
- Create a topic sentence.

Here is an example of how summarizing works:

Original: As children, boys and girls have hemispheric differences. Generally, the female brain develops with a larger left hemisphere. Males start out as young boys with a larger right hemisphere. The implications of this are interesting. As I stated earlier, we know that women tend to be more verbal than men are. In fact, female toddlers have a much larger vocabulary than the boys their age. If we look again at the functions of the two hemispheres, this all makes perfect sense. The left hemisphere has verbal language as one of its functions. If this part of the brain develops earlier in girls, it is no wonder that we surge ahead of the boys in terms of communication skills and vocabulary. A study that was conducted at the University of Buffalo compared the hemispheric differences between male and female infants. Amazingly enough, while the girls were listening and processing language in their left hemispheres, the boys used their right hemispheres. It seemed that the boys didn't begin to use their left hemispheres until 9 months of age. The girls had been making a lot of neural connections in the language areas for months before the boys got started.

Words Deleted: ~~As children, boys and girls have hemispheric differences. Generally~~, *the female brain develops with a larger left hemisphere. Males start out as young boys with a larger right hemisphere.* ~~The implications of this are~~

interesting. ~~As I stated earlier, we know that~~ *women tend to be more verbal than men are. In fact, female toddlers have a much larger vocabulary than the boys their age.* ~~If we look again at the functions of the two hemispheres, this all makes perfect sense.~~ *The left hemisphere has verbal language* ~~as one of its functions. If this part of the brain~~ *develops earlier in girls,* ~~it is no wonder that~~ *we surge ahead of the boys in terms of communication skills and vocabulary.* ~~A study that was conducted at~~ *the University of Buffalo compared the hemispheric differences between male and female infants. Amazingly enough, while the girls were listening and processing language in their left hemispheres, the boys used their right hemispheres.* ~~It seemed that the boys didn't begin to use their left hemispheres~~ *until 9 months of age.* ~~The girls had been making a lot of neural connections in the language areas for months before the boys got started.~~

Summary: *There are differences in brain development in girls and boys. [Note new topic sentence.] The female brain develops with a larger left hemisphere, which has verbal language, while the male brain develops with the right hemisphere larger. This may be the reason that women tend to be more verbal; in fact, female toddlers have a larger vocabulary than boys their age. The University of Buffalo compared the hemispheric differences and found that girls listen and process language in their left hemisphere, while boys use their right until the age of 9 months.*

Your students may benefit from taking a famous oration such as Martin Luther King Jr.'s "I Have a Dream" speech and summarizing sections with partners or groups to help them understand the process. Asking students to read a nonfiction selection from a text and creating an appropriate title also falls into this category.

Summarizing is not a simple task for most students. The better they know and understand the content, the easier it is to summarize. Summary frames, such as those devised by Marzano and colleagues (2001), present common patterns in the form of questions. They cover narratives, topic-restriction-illustration, definition, argumentation, problem or solution, and conversation.

Inferring. *Inferring* is the ability to come to a conclusion based on evidence. As a language arts teacher, I always found this cognitive process to be one of the more difficult ones to teach—and it was always assessed on our state test. In language arts, the *theme* is the universal idea that the author is trying to share with the reader. Themes are rarely revealed in written form—they must be inferred. I found it helpful to differentiate between facts and inferences. *Facts* are observable; *inferences* are interpretations that may remain unresolved.

Students must learn to "read between the lines" to make inferences. A three-column chart may be used as a graphic organizer for inference, with the first column labeled "Facts" or "What I Know for Sure," the middle column designated "Questions" or "What I Wonder," and the third column marked "Inferences." The inferences column may have statements that begin with *maybe* or *probably*. A two-column chart with the labels "Facts" (or "What I Can Observe or Know") and "Inferences" (or "My Interpretation") will also suffice. Students enjoy doing detective work, so presenting inferences in that context may be a good approach to the topic. Marzano and colleagues (2001) suggest using inferential questions such as the following to fill in gaps: "What particular emotional state does this person have?" "Where does this event usually take place?" and "How is this thing usually used?"

Tovani (2000) recommends that we teach students to distinguish between opinions and an inference before proceeding. Opinions may be based on fact, but we cannot assume so, and they aren't sufficient for interpreting text. Ask students what words help them draw a conclusion. Define the following terms:

- *Prediction*: Logical guess based on facts confirmed or disproved by the text.
- *Inference*: Logical conclusion based on text clues and background knowledge.
- *Assumption*: Fact or statement that is taken for granted but that may or may not be correct.
- *Opinion*: Belief or conclusion not based on facts that can be knowledgeable or ridiculous because it is based on what one thinks and isn't verified.

Harvey and Goudvis (2007) suggest playing charades with students to help them understand inference. Discussing and reading body language and visual expressions are also helpful for students.

Comparing. Identifying similarities and differences is the *number one way* to raise student achievement, according to the results of a meta-analysis by Marzano (1998). The study concluded that explicitly guiding students as they identify similarities and differences, asking them to identify similarities and differences independently, and representing similarities and differences in graphic or symbolic form enhances students' understanding of and ability to use knowledge.

To be effective at comparing, students need to be able to see the defining characteristics on which to base the similarities and the differences. The graphic organizer commonly used for this strategy is the Venn diagram (see Appendix B). I used to encourage my students to visualize these diagrams when thinking. The similarities are written in the center, where the circles overlap; the differences or distinguishing characteristics are placed in the parts of each circle that do not intersect.

Metaphors and analogies also help students make comparisons. Both take an unfamiliar concept and equate it with a familiar one. I would begin teaching metaphors with a line from Shakespeare: "All the world's a stage." This metaphor is comparing two unlike items: the world and a stage. My students would work together using a Venn diagram to discover how the two items are similar and different.

The most powerful metaphors are those that students create themselves. I find asking students to follow these steps effective:

- Choose a topic that you know a lot about.
- Define both the topic you are learning in class and the topic that you know a lot about.
- Determine how the two topics are alike in the literal sense (e.g., the weather and computers are both very changeable).
- Determine how they are alike in more theoretical terms (e.g., the weather can affect whether computers can be used).

Metaphoric teaching can help students identify what they do not understand. Metaphors and analogies emphasize relationships and help students recognize and understand patterns. Idioms and similes can also help students organize and connect information (Richards, 2003).

Analogies are usually set up as "A is to B as C is to D," or "A:B::C:D." Those of us who had to take the Miller Analogies Test are quite familiar with the concept. We want to create a statement that suggests that two things are related to each other in the same way that two other things are related to each other (e.g., fish:swim::bird:fly). There are many different types of analogies, covering all content areas:

- Synonyms (Mother:Mom::Father:Dad)
- Antonyms (Inhale:Exhale::Stop:Go)
- Definition (Box:Container constructed with four sides::Ball:Spherical object)
- Object to function (Pen:Write::Car:Drive)
- Part to whole (Tongue:Mouth::Head:Body)
- Type or example (Flu:Illness::Volvo:Car)
- Location (Paris:France::Book:Library)
- Components (Cake:Batter::Computer:Chips)

Research suggests that students' ability to use analogies is related to their working memory capacity. What is very exciting about this research is that very young children can learn information using analogies (Singer-Freeman, 2003).

Metaphoric teaching can help students identify what they do not understand. Metaphors and analogies emphasize relationships and help students recognize and understand patterns. Idioms and similes can also help students organize and connect information (Richards, 2003).

Explaining. Cause and effect are essential elements of explaining. Upon being given a description of a system, students develop and use a cause-and-effect model to assess its components and their relationship to one another. Cause-and-effect relationships can be expressed in if-then statements ("If you are exposed to a flu virus, then you may get the flu," "If you talk on your cell phone while driving, then you may have an accident"). Common connective words include *influence*, *changes*, *why*, *cause*, *effect*, *as a result*, *because of*, *the reason for*, *consequence*, and *decrease*.

Students are naturally curious and want to know why things happen. They can set up their recoding by starting with the effect and then exploring the cause ("Peter is angry because Michael told a lie") or by starting with the cause ("Michael told Peter a lie, so Peter is angry").

Much of the content that we teach involves cause-and-effect principles. Nothing happens without a reason. We often ask questions that refer to cause-and-effect relationships by using the phrase "What happens" ("What happens when you pour lemon juice into a glass of milk?" "What happens if you make noise in a library?" "What happens if you eat too much?"). T-charts are useful as graphic organizers for describing cause-and-effect relationships.

....

Mental Note: Students create their own memories when they recode new material.

....

Recoding Procedural Knowledge

The purpose of recoding is to ascertain whether students understand what they're supposed to be learning. Say you've introduced a procedure and your students have had some time to reflect. Now you want them to recode the procedure—to put it in their own terms to be sure that they understand the concepts behind it. For instance, if you use the following procedure to solve story problems in math—

1. What is the question?
2. What are the important facts?
3. Do you have enough information to solve the problem?
4. Do you have too much information?
5. What operation will you use?
6. Label your answer.
7. Is your answer reasonable?

—then perhaps students could apply a problem to the procedure to see how each step works. If their recoded steps don't solve the problem, they may want to make some changes. This approach may work for science and other content area procedures as well.

Decision making is another procedure that we encourage students to master. Students may use the following steps to guide them:

1. Define a problem.
2. Establish goals and objectives.
3. Define criteria for selection.
4. Gather relevant information.
5. Identify feasible alternatives.
6. Predict future consequences.
7. Compare alternatives.
8. Select the best alternative.

According to Crannell (1994), "Professional mathematicians spend most of their time writing: communicating with colleagues, applying for grants, publishing papers, writing memos and syllabi. Writing well is extremely important to mathematicians, since poor writers have a hard time getting published, getting attention from the deans, and obtaining funding. It is ironic but true that most mathematicians spend more time writing than they spend doing math." Crannell suggests applying the following steps to mathematical writing:

1. Clearly restate the problem to be solved.
2. State the answer in a complete sentence that stands on its own.
3. Clearly state the assumptions that underlie the formulas.
4. Provide a paragraph that explains how the problem will be approached.
5. Clearly label diagrams, tables, graphs, or other visual representations of the math (if these are indeed used).
6. Define all variables used.
7. Explain how each formula is derived, or where it can be found.
8. Give acknowledgment where it is due.
9. Assess whether spelling, grammar, and punctuation are all correct.
10. Assess whether the math correct.

11. Consider whether the writer solved the question that was originally asked.

Sousa (2016) says to think of writing as a kinesthetic activity that engages neurons while communicating math concepts. The writing also helps students organize their thoughts.

Writing across the curriculum is an important component to creating good writers. Research strongly supports the fact that students reinforce their learning when they write about concepts, facts, or procedures. As Cooke (1991) puts it, "When we ask our students to write . . . we are encouraging them to engage actively with the subject matter in our disciplines: to see patterns, connect ideas, make meanings—in other words, to learn" (p. 5).

The research is clear: discipline-based instruction in reading and writing enhances student achievement in all subjects. Studies show that reading and writing across the curriculum are essential to learning. Without strategies for reading course material and opportunities to write thoughtfully about it, students have difficulty mastering concepts.

Mental Note: Students must understand the concepts underlying the procedures they learn to make the information transferable.

Recoding Using Nonlinguistic Representations

Nonlinguistic representations are those that do not rely on words, such as kinesthetic activity, drawn pictures, and graphic representations. Basically, students take semantic information and make it nonsemantic. Many researchers believe that we always store information in both language and images. In their research, Dean, Hubbell, Pitler, and Stone (2012) found that use of graphic organizers yield a percentile gain in student achievement of up to 40 percent.

Some students may opt to recode by drawing pictures, creating models, or moving around. Using the T-chart is useful for this approach. On the left side, students show semantically what they know or understand; on the right side, they draw representative pictures or symbols. Kenyon (2002) found that another graphic organizer, mind mapping, is an especially effective strategy for students with dyslexia when used with nonlinguistic elements.

Once your students have recoded nonlinguistically, they should try to recode using words. Because recoding assists in conceptual understanding, once a concept is understood, transferring to the semantic pathway offers beneficial practice for assessment purposes.

Manipulating Information in Working Memory

The process of recoding gives the brain the time and opportunity to start making connections. When students can state facts, concepts, and procedures in their own words, ownership of the material begins.

Of course, some of our students may lack necessary background knowledge or simply don't "get" what we presented. This is frustrating for all and often based on misunderstandings about content. The longer misunderstandings persist, the harder they are to shake (Bailey & Pransky, 2014), so it is vital to address them as soon as they're discovered.

Recoding needs to take place in the classroom. Sending students home with new material to recode may be stressful. This is not the time for homework and practice; rather, this is the time to ask questions and iron out wrinkles in thinking. At this point in the seven-step process, students have just gone through a reflective period and are "trying out" the material. The opportunity to manipulate new knowledge in working memory is the beginning of setting up neural connections in the brain that, if accurate, will be rehearsed to become lasting long-term memories.

Reflection

1. Consider your current practice. Is recoding always a process you include? How can you incorporate it into your lessons?
2. Examine the recoding practices you have been using. Are you more comfortable with some than others? Step out of your comfort zone and introduce your students to as many of these research-based strategies as you can.

3. You can make the process of recoding as simple or as elegant as you like. I often used small whiteboards. I would ask students to write down whatever they learned about a topic, then walk around the room and check for understanding in a matter of minutes. Then, I might have the students find a partner and compare what they wrote. This little bit of reciprocal teaching usually cleared up any misunderstandings.

4. One of my favorite strategies is called "Show to Tell": Simply ask students to draw a picture of the topic! This is a well-used strategy for vocabulary. Below, a 2nd grader portrays her understanding of the word *nestle*.

Rebecca Alber (2014) suggests quick writes, stop and jots, one-minute essays, and graffiti conversations for training students to recode:

• Quick writes ask students to respond to a prompt within a limited time (2 to 10 minutes).

- In stop and jots, students jot down their own thoughts, pair with a partner to exchange ideas, and then share their ideas with the rest of the class.
- One-minute essays are often used at the beginning of class to get students thinking. These are especially good if you began a new concept on the previous day and want to see what students remember.
- Graffiti conversations are in response to a content-specific prompt (quote, question, image, etc.) and require students to collect their thoughts on paper in words, images, or a combination of the two in order to make their thinking visible. Students work individually to respond, but once they have recorded their thoughts, they can verbally share their reflections or circulate and read the responses of their peers. Graffiti can be recorded on bulletin boards, whiteboards, paper tablecloths, or sidewalks (using sidewalk chalk).

Reinforce

Effective feedback begins with clearly defined and clearly communicated learning goals.

—*Robert Marzano*

I remember observing a prekindergarten classroom as part of my job for the state board of education. Although I started my teaching career at the preK level, it had been many years since I'd worked with students so young. The teacher, Mrs. Keene, was playing a familiar game with the kids that I remembered from my childhood: "Hot and Cold." One child is "it" and is asked to leave the room. The class chooses an object. When the child returns, the class sings a song, getting louder when the child is "hot," or close to the object, or singing softly when the child is "cold," or far from the object.

As I watched the class, I thought of the possible purposes of the game. Certainly the children must be making decisions about when to get louder or softer. Self-control is challenged as the little ones want to point or give other clues as to the selected article. What I found particularly interesting was the feedback that the singing provided. This reinforcement was offered continually. The children did not get frustrated as they searched for the target. Through this use of continuous feedback, every child is successful.

On my second visit, an interesting turn of events occurred as the students played the game: A child from the kindergarten class walked into the room to give Mrs. Keene a note. He had been in Mrs. Keene's class last year and remembered the game.

"I'm going to play, too," the kindergartner announced. "Tell me when I'm hot or cold or getting warmer."

The students complied, but there was a problem: the boy was not present when the object, a red Lego block, was picked, so no matter how "hot" he got, he had to randomly guess at what the object might be. His frustration was evident, and he quit before he could select the red Lego block. After the student left, Mrs. Keene took the time to explain to her class why the game didn't work for her former student. She gave examples of how goals and targets help us accomplish what we are after.

Reinforcement, the act of encouraging and strengthening, is dependent on clear goals and targets. Once our students have recoded the material to help them with their conceptual and procedural understandings, it is time for feedback. In the simplest terms, we are asking the age-old question, "Do they get it?" If not, we must determine what it is they don't get and how we can lead them to understanding.

What Is Reinforcement?

Northwest Regional Educational Laboratory (NWREL, 2002) defines *reinforcement* as providing a verbal or symbolic reward for academic performance or effort. Feedback as reinforcement offers encouragement and the opportunity to fortify what students understand. We can let our students know whether their perceptions and understanding are correct and, if necessary, we can reshape or reteach. Feedback also allows students to change their conceptual understandings before they rehearse for long-term memory.

We want to be able to ascertain whether our students understand what they're learning so far. Once we know that they do, we want to strengthen that understanding and start the process of permanent storage. This is not the time for delivering grades. This is only the launch of students' learning. Reinforcement provides time in working memory to make necessary changes. In other words, information must be "perfect" before it enters permanent storage.

Does instructional reinforcement raise student achievement? Teachers who routinely provide feedback and reinforcement regarding student learning improve results. The reinforcement step is always dependent on an academic goal. These teachers make use of peer evaluation techniques, provide computer-assisted instructional activities that give students immediate feedback regarding their learning performance, assign homework that is corrected and returned promptly—either in class by the students or later by the teacher—and use peer tutoring strategies that include training students to provide each other with feedback and reinforcement (NWREL, 2002).

> ☀ **Mental Note: This is not time for a grade. This is only the launching of student learning.**

Feedback is effective if it "feeds forward" (Moss & Brookhart, 2009, pp. 44–59)—if it "is used by the learner in improving performance" (Wiliam, 2011, p. 120). Van der Kleij, Feskens, and Eggen (2015) found that elaborate feedback—that is, feedback that concentrates on evidence of what students were thinking and not merely about whether their answers were correct—leads to more improvement in learning than simple knowledge of results. Explanations, therefore, are more effective than simple acknowledgements that answers are correct (or providing the answer). These findings apply principally to higher-order learning.

> ☀ **Mental Note: "Failure grows the brain by adding myelin."**
> —*Daniel Coyle*

According to Hattie (2012), "For feedback to be effective, teachers need to clarify the goal of the lesson or activity, ensure that students understand the feedback, and seek feedback from students about the effectiveness of their instruction. The aim of feedback is to reduce the gap between where students are and where they should be. The teacher, therefore, needs to know what students bring to each lesson at the start and to articulate what success looks like."

Types of Feedback

Feedback comes in many forms and from many different sources. Students receive feedback from teachers, classmates, and even themselves. Grades are a form of feedback, but at this step in the memory-building process, students are not ready to be graded. In fact, it is still too soon for homework—but this *is* the time for assessment. As Rick Stiggins (2017) says, "In formative and assessment [for] learning situations, there is no role for grades and numerical test scores. Rather, students need continuous access to descriptive feedback that describes their work and informs them about how to do better next time" (p. 79).

Chappuis, Stiggins, Chappuis, & Arter (2011) speak of two kinds of assessment: assessment *of* learning and assessment *for* learning. Assessment *for* learning includes a continual effort to provide feedback in every part of the lesson. Just as reflection is needed every step of the way for long-term retention, so too is reinforcement. To improve memory, feedback increases interest to keep students on task, and it allows for adjustments. Higbee (1996) reports that when 1st grade students in a study were taught a rehearsal strategy to help them remember material, only those who received feedback on how well it worked continued to use it.

 Mental Note: It is still too soon for homework, but this *is* the time for assessment.

The National Education Association (2003) notes that achievement gains are maximized when educators increase the accuracy of classroom assessments, provide students with frequent informative feedback (versus infrequent or merely judgmental feedback), and involve students deeply in the classroom assessment, recordkeeping, and communication processes.

Strong (2007) came to several important conclusions from his study of ongoing feedback in the classrooms of effective teachers. These teachers, he found,

- Use pre-assessments to support targeted teaching of skills.
- Implement good monitoring strategies by directing questions to the lesson's targets.
- Think through likely misconceptions that students may have and monitor them to look for those misconceptions.
- Give clear, specific, and timely feedback throughout the teaching and learning process.
- Provide feedback in a supportive and encouraging manner.
- Reteach material to students who do not achieve mastery.

☀ **Mental Note: Good practice with effective feedback makes perfect.**

Connellan (2003) describes three types of feedback: *motivational feedback* to accelerate improvement, *informational feedback* that gives students a way to measure progress, and *developmental feedback* to help those students who are underperforming. Each of these types of feedback is useful in the classroom and helps with reinforcement. We need to value all forms of feedback and possibly use them all together.

☀ **Mental Note: Feedback provides the reinforcement students need to remain motivated.**

Motivation and the Brain

Motivation has long been associated with the release of the neurotransmitter dopamine. This chemical has several purposes. One is to help students focus through its release in the frontal lobe. Another is in the brain's reward system. Some believe that dopamine is released when someone accomplishes something (Hamid et al., 2016), though others disagree (see Panskepp &

Biven, 2012). Other research suggests that dopamine is released as a seeking mechanism (Gregory & Kaufeldt, 2015) to initiate a task.

In one of my first workshops with Eric Jensen, he shared the following scenario as a way of explaining the effects of dopamine. Let's say you give your children airline tickets to Disney World as a Christmas present. The excitement is palpable. As the trip approaches, all your kids can think about is Disney World. The dopamine is rushing through their brains and bodies from the moment they received the tickets until the moment finally arrives. The dopamine is now rushing as your family boards the plane, lands in Orlando, deplanes, drives over to the Magic Kingdom, walks in, and—it's not as exciting as they thought. They have achieved their goal, and now the dopamine magic has waned.

Dopamine is the "run, see, go, do!" chemical. For the purposes of learning, it gets students recoding content. If dopamine drives us toward our goal but diminishes upon accomplishment, we must help students replace that chemical with another. It appears that feedback will touch the pride or power area in the brain and release serotonin and endorphins. These provide a wonderful feeling that students want to feel again. As Sinek (2014) puts it, "The more respect and recognition we receive, the higher our status in the group and the more incentive we have to continue to give to the group" (p. 59). They can then be spurred on to the next goal, promoting dopamine release and the beginning of a new cycle.

Motivational States

Jensen (2013) refers to frames of mind as *motivational states*. Any combination of attitudes and beliefs, emotions, and sensations can change from moment to moment. It is up to us as classroom leaders to recognize these states and, if necessary, change them to be more receptive to learning.

Many students enter our classrooms in the same state day after day. Optimistic students are usually upbeat and open to something new; angry students are often scowling; apathetic students seem bored all the time. The optimistic student is in the right frame of mind, but the angry and apathetic students need to change if they are to learn successfully. Some states in which we want to see our students include anticipation, curiosity, intrigue, and suspense.

The quickest thing you can do to alter a student's motivational state is to create a sudden physiological change. For example, if you have a student who is disinterested and sleepy, get his body moving quickly: "Jamal, I need these papers delivered next door in a hurry! And when you get back, could you please help me pass back yesterday's exit cards? We have a lot to do!" When the student is up and moving, dopamine, adrenaline, and a little cortisol are released in the brain. And as he's working on the task you've given him, be sure to prepare work for him to complete as the dopamine diminishes. Acknowledge the student's help to the class as a way of engaging serotonin receptors: "Class, today is brought to you by the helpful movements of Jamal. Without his assistance this morning, we would not be able to reach our goals. Let's give Jamal our gratitude." The release of both dopamine and serotonin in this scenario will push the student to seek new learning, stay involved with his classmates, and even want to help more in class!

> ☀ **Mental Note: The type of feedback you use, as well as your timing and your method, can alter your students' motivational state.**

Immediate feedback is usually preferable during the recoding process. Because feedback is essential for knowing whether students are ready to move on, waiting to deliver it can be detrimental to long-term memory. Interactive feedback helps students to more comprehensively understand what they're learning. Written feedback makes more of a difference on formative than on summative assessments, as students may not pay as much attention to feedback accompanying an already settled grade. Feedback on formative assessments offers students the opportunity to make changes and feel in control of their learning.

Mental Note: "Feedback should be an episode of learning for both student and teacher." —*Susan Brookhart*

Motivational Feedback

Motivational feedback can be divided into three distinct forms: *positive feedback, negative feedback,* and what Connellan (2003) calls *extinction.* Positive feedback reinforces good or correct behavior, negative feedback addresses poor or incorrect behavior, and extinction is the complete lack of any feedback at all. Goleman (1998) cites research showing that students who don't receive any feedback on their actions suffer the same loss of self-confidence as those who receive negative feedback.

As much as possible, we want to share positive feedback with our students —feedback that cheers them on to peak performance. Whereas positive feedback helps create a virtuous cycle in which "good" chemicals like adrenaline, norepinephrine, dopamine, and serotonin are released in students' brains, negative feedback or no feedback at all flood them instead with the stress hormone cortisol and with other neurotransmitters, interrupting thinking by taking over working memory (Sandi, 2013).

 Mental Note: There are three types of motivational feedback: positive, negative, and absent (extinction).

Positive Feedback

Positive feedback is the reinforcement that makes students want to keep doing what they've been doing. Connellan (2003) offers five principles of positive feedback:

1. **Reinforce immediately.** Immediate feedback does not have to be instantaneous; it may sometimes take you a little time to check a student's recoded material. After all, you are building a framework for further learning. If you have the ability to cruise the room as students

recode material, you may be able to offer feedback verbally. How about using the power of touch, too? A literal pat on the back can work wonders for some students.

2. **Reinforce any improvement, not just excellence.** In our fast-paced educational environment, it is easy to overlook the baby steps that some students take toward understanding. We are programmed to look for bottom lines and have been trained to seek and admire excellence. The truth is that some students may only be scratching the surface in their recoding efforts. To assist our students on their journey to building long-term memory, we must let them acquire awareness in bits and pieces. Any improvement you detect in your students is worthy of positive feedback.

3. **Be specific in your reinforcement.** Teachers are often very general in their positive comments: "Good description!" "Nice comparisons." When it comes to finding faults, however, we can be very specific. It is common to start with positive feedback in general before zeroing in on details with negative feedback: "I like the graphic organizer you chose for this concept, but a Venn diagram can't be used this way. You can't put contrasting information in the middle, and you are wasting space by writing the similarities twice in the outside areas." A better approach might be to be encouraging in your specificity: "I can tell that you are really trying to gain an understanding of this concept. Let's look at what you have here. Your mind map may need some revision. Your first major detail needs more support. Your second and third details have interesting symbols, and you might want to add a few key words or phrases here. The last detail is your best; it is very clear that you understand this part."

4. **Continuously reinforce positive new behaviors,** such as using new types of organizers, taking new approaches to recoding, or improving in any way.

5. **Intermittently reinforce good habits.** Once new behaviors become habits, students may be able to reinforce them on their own, so we can draw back and reinforce them less often.

Mental Note: Because students may only be scratching the surface of their recoding efforts, we should offer positive feedback on any improvement we detect.

 Mental Note: Give positive feedback to students who are making small gains.

Negative Feedback

Colbert and Knapp (2000) suggest the following six steps for addressing issues that need correcting:

1. Focus the evaluation.
2. Point out the original goals.
3. Identify responsibility.
4. Communicate specific components.
5. Discuss a new plan of action.
6. Confirm correct results.

The following example shows each of these steps in action:

As the students identify similarities and differences of Civil War generals, Mrs. Ling circulates and glances at her students' Venn diagrams. When she reaches Carmen's desk, she sees that Carmen has recoded her material as a paragraph.

Mrs. Ling asks, "Carmen, are you going to create your graphic organizer from the paragraph?" (Step 1)

"I like to write in sentences," Carmen responds.

"The instructions are to create a Venn diagram showing the similarities in the overlapping areas of the circles and the differences in the outer areas. (Step 2) Look at the one on the overhead. Your job is to show me that you can use a Venn diagram properly. (Step 3) Do you understand that you must include characteristics of the

generals that are alike and those that are different? (Step 4) Below your paragraph, draw the graphic organizer. (Step 5) That's right. Fill it in with some of that information from your paragraph and I'll come back to check on you." (Step 6)

Another option is to employ *Socratic dialogue.* This process involves asking several categories of questions: clarification questions, questions about the initial question or issue, assumption probes, reason and evidence probes, origin or source questions, implication and consequence probes, and viewpoint questions. Sample questions from Paul (1993) are provided in Figure 4.1.

Socratic questioning allows us to guide students to the correct destination themselves. The questions keep the students on track to develop a conceptual understanding of the material. Questioning strategies may build upon each other, or they may simply lead the teacher and students on a more random journey that ends with a positive outcome. Socratic dialogue helps students to fully explore the depth and breadth of their understanding. When I started using this method with students in the 1980s, I found it challenging at first, but students soon began to thank me for sticking with them.

The following scenario shows the effective use of Socratic dialogue in the classroom:

Students have just finished recoding their new material on Shirley Jackson's "The Lottery." The unit thus far has consisted of the following steps:

Reach and Teach: *When the students entered the room on the first day of the lesson, Ms. Brown was folding small white pieces of paper and placing them in a box. As soon as they took their seats, she began.*

"Class, I ordered tickets to the play based on the story we are about to read, Shirley Jackson's 'The Lottery,' she announced. "There are 27 students in the class, so I asked for 28 tickets to include me. Unfortunately, they mailed only 27 tickets. When I called, they said the play was completely sold out. So, to be fair about this, I have put 27 blank pieces of paper in this box. I also put one piece in it that is marked with an x. We will all take turns drawing from the box. The person who gets the x will be unable to go to the theater with us and will instead go to another English class." The students were curious about the process. Everyone drew from the

FIGURE 4.1	Socratic Questions Adapted from the Work of Richard Paul (1993)
Type of Question	**Examples**
Clarification Questions	• What do you mean by…? • What is your main point? • How does _____ relate to_____? • Could you put that another way? • Can you give me an example?
Questions About the Question	• How can we find out? • Is the question clear? • Why is this question important? • To answer this question, what would we have to answer first?
Assumption Probes	• What are you assuming? • What could we assume instead? • Why would someone make this assumption?
Reason and Evidence Probes	• What would be an example? • How do you know? • What led you to that belief? • What would change your mind? • How does that apply to this case?
Origin or Source Questions	• Where did you get this idea? • Have you always felt this way? • What effect would that have? • What is an alternative?
Implication and Consequence Probes	• If this is true, what else should also be true? • What would be the effect?
Viewpoint Questions	• How would other groups respond? • Why have you chosen this perspective? • What would someone who disagrees say?

box, keeping their papers folded until all were finished, then opening them all at the same time.

John received the x. Some of the students snickered. Many breathed a sigh of relief. No one questioned the teacher's authority to have a lottery. John said it wasn't fair. He didn't deserve to be left out. After all, he was a good student. "Someone who doesn't work hard should be left out," he complained.

Reflect: After revealing that there actually were 28 tickets, the teacher placed students into groups for a four-corner reflection. She posted one of the following questions to each corner:

1.   How do you feel about this lottery?
2.   How could this decision have been made fairly?
3.   How do your peers influence your decision making?
4.   Why were you willing to leave one person out?

The students went from corner to corner discussing each question and adding comments to the sheets.

Recode: The students were then asked to read "The Lottery." Their recoding assignment was to exemplify and list the pros and cons of uncritically following traditions and rituals.

Reinforce: In small-group discussions, students shared their lists. Ms. Brown circulated to offer feedback. At one table, Jess and Robert were arguing.

"You're nuts," Robert said. "Birthday parties are not rituals."

"What do you mean by ritual?" Ms. Brown asked.

"Rituals are things you do over and over," Robert replied.

"Can you give me an example?"

"Yeah, like going to church."

"What elements of church make it a ritual?"

"You know, you go and they do the same stuff all the time. The service follows the same pages in the book. The people sing the same hymns. They go every Sunday. That's a ritual," Robert declared.

"What are you assuming about birthday parties?"

"Birthday parties are different every time. You can go to a movie or have a big party or do nothing," he replied.

"What is Jess saying to you that you don't agree with?" she probed.

"Jess says that birthdays are rituals because you are celebrating the day you were born each year, and that you have cake and ice cream, and you get cards."

"How do birthdays once a year relate to going to church, Robert?"

He thought for several moments. The teacher gave him the wait time even though others in his group had their hands up and wanted to answer.

Robert said, "I think I can see it now. Once a year or once a week, the same basic concept is being replayed. OK, I think I understand rituals better now."

The Socratic questioning technique allowed Robert to come to his own conclusions in this scenario. Ms. Brown provided the feedback that would change his understanding of the concept and give him a greater chance of storing correct information in long-term memory.

Extinction

My son Josh walked in after school and quietly put his books down. His sister, Marnie, was doing her homework, and I was working on lesson plans.

"So, how was your day?" I asked, looking up from grading papers.

"Oh, you can see me?" asked Josh.

Surprised, I put my pen down. "Of course I can see you. What kind of question is that?"

"I thought maybe I was invisible," Josh replied.

Thoughts of insanity and drug abuse passed through my mind. "Please explain yourself," I said.

"We had to turn in the outlines for our projects in chemistry," he said. "Mrs. Green walked from table to table and picked up the papers. Gina and Sarah's was first. She looked it over and got a big grin on her face. She said, 'Girls, I think you've got it!' Gina and Sarah were all excited. Then she went to Justin and Jason's table and picked up their outline. She looked at it and got a puzzled look on her face. She said something like, 'Are you sure you two understand what an outline is supposed to look like?' Boy, were they embarrassed. She came to my table next. She picked up our outline, looked at it, and didn't say a word. I couldn't even see an expression on her face. It was like Dan and I didn't even exist."

"How did she react to the other kids' papers?"

"I don't know. She looked at a few, and then the bell rang. Everyone had to turn the papers in quickly."

Marnie piped in. "At least she didn't say anything negative about yours."

"Are you kidding?" Josh barked. "Negative would have been better than nothing!"

"Well, I'm sure she'll give you some feedback," I said.

"You don't get it, Mom—she did give me feedback! She told me my work didn't matter!"

That conversation got me thinking about the way I responded to my students in class. How many times had I made some of them feel invisible? I remembered what my principal said to me: "My job is to bring out the best in people. That's your job, too." Mrs. Green certainly wasn't bringing out the best in Josh, but I bet she was like me and didn't have a clue what she had done.

My children happened to have the same English teacher in high school. We still make jokes about the papers that she never handed back. It can be funny to us now, but it wasn't funny to her students back then. They would work very hard on papers and never get any type of feedback. Let's give her the benefit of the doubt—she had between 100 and 150 students each day. That's a lot of papers to grade. But she didn't have to grade every one of them. It is OK to assign work and not grade it, but you should always provide feedback on recoding.

Students can assess themselves and assess each other. If you are having students share their initial recoding, working in cooperative groups may be timely and helpful. A sharing of the recoded material followed by a discussion may clarify some concepts. This approach also gives you time to cruise the room and listen to each group. You may then want to collect this first attempt at recoding to quickly review for the next day, assessing whether to add more material, reteach, or move on to the rehearsal stage.

You can use Pearson and Gallagher's (1983) gradual release of responsibility (GRR) model to frame your feedback. There are four steps to the model:

1. The teacher completes a task, demonstrating the steps for students.
2. The teacher and students complete the task together.
3. The students complete the task together.

4. Each student completes the task alone.

A rubric like the one in Figure 4.2 can be helpful for teaching students to evaluate their work using the GRR model. You would begin by providing students with feedback using the rubric, which helps them to understand it. The next time, both the teacher and the students discuss and assess their work together. Once they've got the hang of providing feedback, they work in pairs to do so on one another's work. Finally, students can begin evaluating their own work themselves.

FIGURE 4.2	A Rubric for Feedback on Recoded Material
4. The student has completely recoded the information and can explain his self-generated information effectively	
3. The student has recoded most of the information and can explain his self-generated information.	
2. The student has recoded some of the information and has a vague understanding.	
1. The student has recoded little or none of the information and cannot be said to understand the topic.	

Mental Note: Students benefit from providing feedback to other students.

Mental Note: "Feedback is not about praise or blame, approval or disapproval. That's what evaluation is— placing value. Feedback is value-neutral. It describes what you did and did not do."—*Grant Wiggins*

Informational Feedback

Whereas motivational feedback acts to hasten improvement, *informational feedback* offers students a visual representation of progress. According to Connellan (2003), informational feedback should be *goal oriented, immediate,* and *graphic*.

1. **Goal oriented:** Gone are the days of keeping goals and objectives from students. If you are teaching students writing strategies that emphasize organization, show them examples of essays with good organizational qualities.

2. **Immediate:** A meta-analysis of reinforcement studies (Cotton, 2000) found that offering immediate feedback is especially important for younger students. Marzano, Pickering, and Pollack (2001) found that the most powerful informational feedback includes a verbal or written explanation of what was accurate and inaccurate in student responses.

3. **Graphic:** Charts, graphs, diagrams, and simple symbols can all be very effective methods of providing informational feedback. Crossland and Clarke (2002) firmly promote the use of graphics and symbols with every written communication to students (see Figure 4.3).

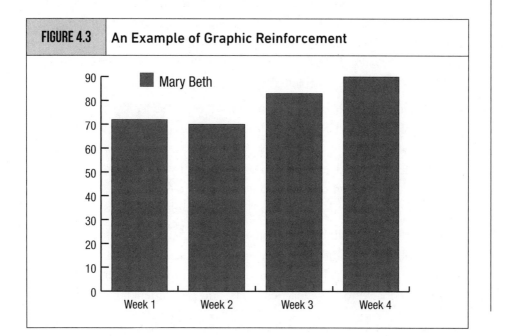

FIGURE 4.3   **An Example of Graphic Reinforcement**

According to Dweck (2006), teachers should focus on student efforts rather than their abilities. Focusing on individual intelligence just puts more pressure on students. Feedback that emphasizes effort and learnable strategies provides students the incentive to take on new challenges.

In one study, researchers divided 128 5th graders into groups and gave them a simple IQ test. The first group were told they did really well and must be really smart. The second group were told they did really well and must have worked hard. One group was praised for intelligence, the other for effort. Asked if they wanted to take a slightly harder test, the kids praised for their intelligence were reluctant. Of those praised for their effort, however, 90 percent were eager for a more challenging task. On a final test, the group praised for effort performed significantly better than the group praised for intelligence. Many of the kids who had been labeled "smart" performed worst of all. The "hard workers" got the message that they could improve their scores by trying harder, but the "smart" kids believed they should do well without any effort (Mueller & Dweck, 1998).

There does not appear to be a lot of research suggesting that praise alone helps students learn (Hattie & Yates, 2014). Praise can make students feel happy, but it is constructive feedback that increases knowledge. Some even believe that praise can inhibit learning by encouraging students to focus on seeking it rather than on new learning (Dweck, 2006).

Hattie and Yates (2014) offer the following findings about informational feedback derived from a meta-analysis of relevant studies:

- It is important to assess how students receive the feedback.
- Feedback should prompt the learner toward the task but away from himself.
- Feedback should engage learners at or slightly above their level.
- The learning environment should be open to errors.
- Peer feedback using respectful rules is valuable.

Report cards contain informational feedback, but it's often too little, too late. Portfolios are another way of bringing curriculum, instruction, and assessment together. Without formal grades, a portfolio may contain informational feedback from the teacher, peers, and the students themselves.

Working portfolios are nontraditional and brain-compatible forms of assessment that may show growth over time. Application of concepts may be easier to observe through portfolio samples than through more traditional assessments (Sprenger, 1999).

> ☀ **Mental Note: Many parents desire informational feedback. A visual representation other than the traditional report card may supply them with what they seek.**

Developmental Feedback

Feedback is *developmental* when it affects student performance. As Brookhart (2017) reminds us, oral feedback is very often developmental, especially for younger students who are still learning to read and write. Conventional developmental feedback includes a statement of the problem, followed by some questioning strategies. You want to be sure to provide this sort of feedback before students experience a sense of helplessness. Returning to the class studying "The Lottery," developmental feedback might take the following form:

> **Teacher:** *Sabrina, I see you're using a T-chart. I don't see examples of rituals and traditions. You seem to have characteristics instead.*
> **Sabrina:** *I just don't get this. That story was kind of hard to read.*
> [At this point, try to help the student correct the error or misconception.]
> **Teacher:** *What can you do to adjust this?* [No accusations. No blame.]
> **Sabrina:** *I guess I can't think of any examples.*
> **Teacher:** *Let's take a look at the characteristics you have written down.*
> [Sabrina checks her chart.]
> **Sabrina:** *Traditions are things that people do because other people did them before.*
> **Teacher:** *Can you think of another word for that?*
> **Sabrina:** *No.*

Teacher: Who are the people that were before you?

Sabrina: You mean, like my parents and grandparents?

Teacher: Yes. Did they do anything that you now do?

Sabrina: No.

Teacher: Does your mom do anything that your grandma did?

Sabrina: My mom says it's a custom to hang mistletoe above the front door at Christmas, so you have to kiss everyone who comes in! That is so gross.

Teacher: So, is a custom the same thing as tradition?

Sabrina: I guess so.

[Now is the time to reinforce.]

Teacher: Custom is a synonym for tradition. Can you think of another custom?

Sabrina: Well, it's customary in this country to put your hand over your heart when you say the Pledge of Allegiance.

Teacher: I think you have the idea now. That's another example. See if you can think of more. I'll be back to check on you.

The process above consists of five steps:

1. Describe the problem.
2. Invite solutions.
3. Look at options.
4. Call attention to constructive responses.
5. Arrange for further feedback.

Sabrina felt helpless in her situation. She was resistant because she doubted her abilities. Although she tried to blame the story for being too difficult, the teacher could not let her use that excuse. After all, examples of traditions can be constructed without having read the story. The recoding strategy was used to teach the concept of exemplifying, the meaning of tradition and ritual, and the ability to identify similarities and differences. The teacher helped Sabrina in her understanding of these ideas through some reinforcement strategies.

> ☼ **Mental Note: Differentiation is key when providing developmental feedback. Students who require this type of reinforcement may have missed something in the original instruction.**

Feedback Results

Our brains want us to be safe and happy; survival is at the forefront of all that we do. Feedback offers the opportunity to fulfill those needs. The emotional systems for both fear and pleasure are involved as working memory manipulates information and asks for reinforcement.

Through understanding, our students can be successful and feel in control. Emotional areas of the brain are involved in learning situations that include feedback (Zull, 2002). Many memory researchers agree that emotional involvement creates stronger memories (Gordon & Berger, 2003). According to Marzano (1998), a 29-percentile-point difference in student learning can be achieved through frequent feedback.

Butler (1987) studied the effect of different types of feedback on students after an assessment. Some received written comments addressing specific targets that the students were aware of before the assessment (developmental feedback), some received grades alone (informational feedback), and some received grades and comments (a combination of the two). Interestingly, when these students performed two more tasks, those who received comments alone improved their performance significantly. Those who received grades alone declined on the second task, but picked up on the third. The students who received comments and grades declined on the subsequent tasks.

When we reinforce student understanding of learning and are assured they are ready for the next step, we can design appropriate and engaging rehearsal strategies to create long-term, permanent memories.

Reflection

1. Feedback should be timely. Tileston (2004), among others, suggests that feedback be given every 30 minutes. Examine your feedback strategies. What kind of reinforcement could you add?

2. Be sure students know what to do with feedback. It should take them to a very transparent goal and offer suggestions for further achievement.

3. Reinforcement must be specific. This is the time for students to "get it right." Before you send them on to the next step, you want to be sure that homework and practice are possible with their current understanding.

4. Brookhart (2017) suggests using exemplars for students to analyze good work. Think about this best practice. Do you offer your students the opportunity to see models of what you are looking for?

Rehearse

We remember better the more fully we process new subject matter.

—*Larry Squire and Eric Kandel*

I ran across the hall to the 8th grade history teacher's room. I wanted to borrow her globe for a lesson I was going to begin when my students finished writing in their journals. The teacher was in the midst of doing a KWL chart with her class. I stood outside the door for a moment to observe these students, whom I had taught last year.

"What do you know about democracy?" began the teacher. "Let's brainstorm what we know or think we know and write it in the column under K." She paused to give her students some wait time.

Silence filled the room. She glanced at the clock and watched as the second hand went a full 10 seconds. Still no responses.

"So, are you telling me that you know nothing about democracy? How about a definition? Can anyone tell me what democracy is?"

Again, silence.

At this point, I was ready to freak out. These were my students last year. We studied the democratic system. Inside my head I was yelling, "People! Government by the people! Don't you remember? Were you not in my room last year? Did you not take and pass a test on this information? What is wrong with you?" Then my thoughts would turn to my practice: "Or am I a horrible teacher?"

I entered the room at this point to retrieve the globe, hoping that my inter-ruption wouldn't increase thoughts of my incompetence in the teacher's mind. As I

walked to her desk, I noticed some of the students staring at me. Their gazes contin-
ued as I stopped, asked for the globe, and awaited the teacher's response. Suddenly,
several of the students who were looking intently at me raised their hands. One
shouted, "Oh, I remember about democracy! We learned about that last year in
Mrs. Sprenger's room!"

We have all had similar experiences. Students enter our classes at the beginning of the school year, and because we know what was covered the previous years, we assume that they learned and remember. In most cases, they did learn, and after a review, they can retrieve some of the information from long-term memory. When I walked into my colleague's classroom, a number of the students who were looking at me were also searching their memory banks for information about democracy that they had received from me. These experiences were recorded through the episodic pathway. They had not yet "transferred" to the semantic pathway, where they might have been retrieved without my presence. I was the connection to the memory.

We know that in this test-driven world, our students may do well on a classroom assessment yet "forget" the material shortly thereafter. The fact is that you cannot forget something you never truly learned. In the above example, my former students remembered the material only through a specific cue—my barging into the class. Information must be stored in many areas of the brain to make it easily accessible *without* cues. For some students, this so-called transfer rate can take a very long time (Van Blerkom, 2011).

Rehearsal is the step that promotes the storage of information in long-term memory. Many variables interact in preparing information in ways that will make it accessible and transferable. Keep in mind that whenever we have given our students the opportunity to reflect, they have had *some* rehearsal time. Thinking about what they have learned causes them to repeat the information verbally or mentally in their own words.

In this chapter, we will look at the importance of rote and elaborate rehearsal, multiple memory pathways, homework and practice, and, last but not least, sleep. I will incorporate higher levels of thinking into the rehearsal process, as well. Wenglinsky (2002) notes that students of teachers who emphasize higher-order thinking skills in math and hands-on learning activities in science outperform their peers considerably. Using the scientifically based strategies introduced in the recoding stage will also help students remember and raise achievement.

What Is Rehearsal?

Glenn was making me crazy. The kid loved music more than anything else in the world. He was constantly tapping out a beat on his desk or his book. At 11 years old, he had memorized more lyrics than anyone I knew.

It was Tuesday morning, and we were just finishing math. Our next subject was science, where I had recently introduced new vocabulary words and asked students to create a visual or mnemonic device to remember them. As I was trying to determine the best way to share the students' memory aids, I was once again interrupted by Glenn's tapping. I watched as he mouthed some rap lyrics to the beat he tapped out on his desk. Other students were also watching him, some nodding their heads to the rhythm. Some of the girls looked at Glenn as though he were a rap star. Just what every 5th grader needs, I thought. Groupies!

"Glenn, what are you doing?" I asked.

"I'm practicing, Mrs. Sprenger," he replied.

"Well, we're not working on a rap concert for you today," I countered. "We have important vocabulary to cover."

"But that's what I'm doing," he said. "I'm rapping my vocabulary so I can remember it." He proceeded to share his rap on the parts of the heart. It was actually quite good! Several of the students wanted to learn it—they thought it was the best mnemonic they'd ever heard.

You've probably seen another example of mnemonic rehearsal on television. In the commercial, a young man is driving down the street, his head bobbing and his lips moving. Young women see him and appear to be smitten by his coolness. He continues his drive until we, the audience, are finally allowed inside the car to hear what we believe will be a song. Instead, we hear him repeating, over a heavy beat, his grocery list!

Information that enters immediate memory is lost rapidly unless it is manipulated in some way. Rehearsal, a form of such mental manipulation, comes in two types: *rote* and *elaborative*. Rote rehearsal is effective when the information will be used in the same way as it is rehearsed (Sousa, 2017). Multiplication facts, states and capitals, and the order of the presidents are examples of material that can be rehearsed in a rote fashion. Elaborative rehearsal is more useful for teaching semantic information because it relies on creating meaning, and meaningful information is more memorable.

According to Marzano, Pickering, and Pollack (2001), skill learning requires at least 24 practices to reach 80 percent proficiency. The Power Law of Learning (Anderson, 2000), which explains how long it takes to recognize accurately information that has been presented, suggests that it takes many exposures to information for it to be accurately memorized. Each time information is offered, the number of seconds before it is recognized decreases.

Eichenbaum and Dickerson (2010) note that our semantic memories are born out of our episodic memories because we live our lives in episodes. As we derive information from each episode, the information is stored in the brain. The brain takes the repeated bits of information out of the experiences, and those become our semantic memories. An example would be all of the attributes we know about dogs. The fact that dogs wag their tails may have come from several "dog" experiences where we saw this take place. We have heard dogs barking many times, so we may associate this trait with dogs. The experiences themselves may have escaped our memories, so that we no longer know when and where they occurred, but the distinguishing characteristics of the animals stay with us due to repeated exposure. Providing students numerous episodes in which to experience new knowledge is a vital component of elaborative rehearsal. Students will reactivate whatever networks of neurons may have been created in previous episodes of exposure to the new content. Until the memories are consolidated in the brain, they are susceptible to disruption and must be retrieved via the pathway where they were stored. Eventually, the information will become accessible without any specific triggers or cues.

☀ **Mental Note: Memories must be rehearsed in multiple ways to store them in many areas of the brain.**

Why Rehearse?

To *rehearse* is to recite or repeat in private for experimenting and improvement. Students must try out their newfound learning. To help my students understand the idea that concepts and skills must be practiced, I use the following activity. The exercise works best in a large room; I use the library, cafeteria, or gymnasium or take the students outside if the weather is nice. I divide the students into two groups, spreading them out, and give the student closest to the front in each group a beach ball. This person is the "sender." I designate the person in each group who is farthest away as the "receiver." The rules are simple: The beach ball must get to the receiver without the students moving their feet and without the ball touching the ground. Beach balls are so light that most students cannot throw them directly to the target easily. Through trial and error, the students determine what order of tossing the ball to people on the team will work to get it where it's supposed to go.

When the teams have accomplished their task, I look at my watch and say, "Well, both groups got the job done, but that took a long time. Let's try it again!" With a little competition and the clock ticking, the students try to relay the ball faster than before. In some cases, they use fewer people to intercept it. Sometimes the tosses go wild, the ball drops, and they must start over. Eventually, each team figures out how to get the ball to the receiver quickly. At this point, they believe they have finally triumphed.

I take time to discuss the meaning of this activity. The students all had to work together to figure out which method worked best. But had they really learned? In order for the learning to become permanent, they would have to practice this routine over and over. Then tomorrow or next week they could reassemble, and everyone would remember where they stood and to whom the ball should be tossed. Practice sets up networks in their brains.

Marzano, Pickering, and Pollack (2001) cite studies showing that students who practice score between 21 and 44 percent higher on standardized tests than those who don't. This result makes sense, of course, because long-term memories are networks of neurons that have been strengthened through repetition. But to truly ensure mastery, we need our students to practice *past* perfection (Schenck, 2011). As the saying goes, "Don't teach it till they get it right—teach it till they can't get it wrong!" Rehearsal or practice usually ends when students know the answer, but continuing allows them to learn the material in more varied ways to form new associations and to aid retrieval under more diverse circumstances. (Overlearning is especially helpful for students who suffer from text anxiety, which interferes with their ability to recall information. Because information that has been overlearned is so firmly embedded in long-term memory, it is not susceptible to this problem.)

 Mental Note: Some information must be overlearned to become permanent.

What Should Be Rehearsed?

Any knowledge—factual, conceptual, or procedural—that is leading students to their target should be rehearsed. The goal, standard, benchmark, or performance descriptor you are aiming toward requires your students to have some long-term retention of the understanding. Information necessary for both classroom assessments and standardized tests needs to be rehearsed.

As previously noted, some factual and procedural knowledge may be practiced through rote rehearsal. We learn to ride a bike by *trying* to ride a bike—that is, practicing the skill repeatedly until we perfect it.

How Should Rehearsal Be Done?

Rehearsal consists of homework, practice, events, and experiences that will store information in multiple memory pathways. According to Medina (2014), "Repetitions must be spaced out, not crammed in" (p. 150), as doing so makes the memories more vivid. Because memories take a long time to form and can be subject to much interference, students must be re-exposed to information for later recall. The more elaborately they rehearse information, the more details they will remember.

The rehearsal process may use many of the recoding strategies. For example, identifying similarities and differences, a strategy introduced in Chapter 3, has been found to raise student achievement by 25 to 45 percent (Dean et al., 2012). Students who explore similarities and differences have the opportunity to generate their own understanding.

Let's say you want to provide students with multiple episodes in which to rehearse similarities and differences under different circumstances. If you have a self-contained classroom, you may be able to use the strategy across disciplines, as in these examples:

- *Literature:* Read a short story in which two friends are vying for the same trophy. Ask students to create a Venn diagram to show the similarities and differences between the two friends' approaches.
- *Social science:* Compare and contrast the responsibilities of community workers.
- *Math:* Solve a problem using different strategies and then compare the strategies' effectiveness.
- *Music:* Discuss the similarities and differences between songs with comparable messages or melodies.
- *Art:* Compare and contrast artistic styles or media.
- *Other:*
  — Compare the city and the countryside.
  — Draw images of experiences or objects that have both similarities and differences.
  — Perform skits comparing and contrasting two athletes.
  — Students write about two important people in their lives, describing how they are similar and different.

When Is Enough, Enough?

Activities such as the ones above should be preceded by reflection time and followed by reflection and reinforcement after they are completed. The experiences should be spread over a period of weeks, with some being completed in class and others assigned as homework. In between the episodes, students have time to sleep on the information, which helps with memory storage (Diekelmann & Born, 2010; Mateika, Millrood, & Mitru, 2002).

If we could peer into the students' brains, we would see networks being set up (see Figure 5.1).

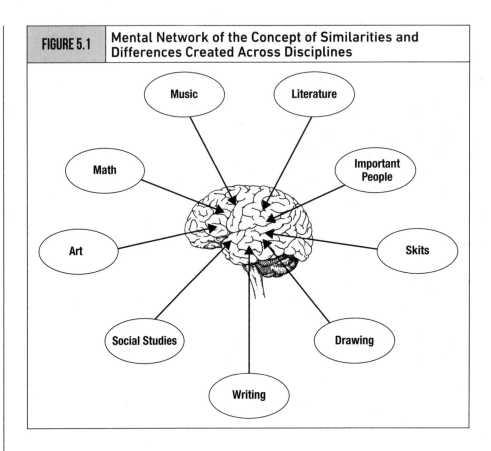

FIGURE 5.1 | Mental Network of the Concept of Similarities and Differences Created Across Disciplines

Music

Literature

Math

Important People

Art

Skits

Social Studies

Drawing

Writing

☀ **Mental Note: Multiple experiences lead to stronger memories.**

Rehearsal and Sleep

Teachers are usually eager to find out about the amount of sleep that their students should be getting. During workshops, almost all raise their hands when I ask if they believe they have students who are sleep deprived. What does sleep have to do with learning?

Many memory researchers agree that memories are encoded during sleep (Mazza et al., 2016). Stickgold and Walker (2013) found that students who slept only six hours after a learning session remembered much less than those who slept a full eight hours. The networks of neurons that form during learning reconnect during the sleeping process.

We all have crammed for an exam at one time or another. We've stayed up late going over our notes, awakened early to go over them again, and looked them over one more time right before the test. Many of us were able to store enough information in working memory to do quite well. But we all know that as soon as the test was over, the information was gone. Of course, we hadn't stored the information in long-term memory—we hadn't had enough sleep to allow our neural connections to strengthen enough. Research suggests that cutting back on sleep reduces the brain's ability to commit new learning to memory and affects attention, mood, reasoning, and general math knowledge (Medina, 2014).

☀ **Mental Note: Cramming is a way to forget rather than remember.**

Homework and Practice

Homework should be time to practice something that has already been learned. After introducing a new skill or concept, the information is in working memory—essentially a fragile holding tank. By the time many students leave the classroom, much of the information in their working memory has disappeared. How can we expect students to take home material to practice when their brains do not have strong enough networks to carry out the task? We can't. According to Wormeli (2014), "If homework is assigned to students before the concepts are clarified . . . then it does more harm than good. Learning acquired from practicing incorrectly is very hard to overcome."

At this point in the seven steps to long-term memory, the students have been introduced to new information (Reach), reflected on it to make connections (Reflect), provided some sort of written proof of their level of understanding (Recode), and received feedback on the material (Reinforce). As we begin the fifth step, we don't simply repeat what we've already introduced, but rather add to it to make it more meaningful and to deepen learning.

According to Stronge (2007), quality, not quantity, is the key to effective homework. Stronge also reports that homework is most effective when it is graded and discussed in class. In the first edition of his book *The Art and Science of Teaching* (2007), Robert Marzano cites research showing that homework is not as effective for younger students as it is for older ones, and that its effectiveness increases by grade: by 6 percent for 4th through 6th grades, 12 percent for 7th through 9th grades, and 24 percent for 10th through 12th grades. The Marzano Center (2013) recommends adding 10 minutes to homework for every grade level. The center also recommends that all homework be directly related to the learning goals for the relevant unit. The assignment should be transparent enough that students understand the correlation between what they are studying and the homework.

In Marzano's (2017) *The New Art and Science of Teaching*, he focuses exclusively on purposeful homework. Oftentimes teachers are either expected to give homework or give homework out of habit. In these cases, the homework has little to do with current goals and content. Marzano states clearly that homework should be given only when needed. He suggests the following conditions for assigning homework:

1. *As a preview*: a short reading or video that provides some knowledge of upcoming content
2. *To deepen knowledge*: comparing current work to other work
3. *To practice a skill*: improving speed, accuracy, and so on after learning a skill
4. *To share with parents*: parents listen to reading, ask questions, assess oral summaries, or work with students on speed or accuracy

Remember, homework is a rehearsal of information on which students show near-mastery. I only give homework if I am sure my students can complete it without any help. Sometimes I ask students to teach what they've learned to someone else at home. If they can teach it, they know it!

Dunlosky, Rawson, Marsh, Nathan, and Willingham (2013) ranked rehearsal strategies according to effectiveness and came to the following conclusions:

- Summarization, highlighting or underlining, using a keyword mne-monic (combining substitute words with visual images), using imagery for text learning (picturing the content of each paragraph as clear and simple images), and rereading were found to be among the least effec-tive strategies.
- Elaborative interrogation (prompting explanations for explicitly stated facts), self-explanation (students explaining some aspect of their learn-ing process), and interleaved practice (alternating practice of different kinds of skills or knowledge) were found to be moderately effective.
- Practice testing and distributed practice (learning distributed over time) were the most effective strategies of all.

I urge you to read Dunlosky and colleagues' study to understand the specif-ics. I am sure many of you are as surprised as I am. The authors found that despite its low ranking, summarization is an important skill to learn, as it helps student to learn and retain material for short periods of time.

O'Keefe (2014) cites a study in which students from the same science class were asked to respond to two different prompts. Half the students were asked to summarize what they had learned in class; the other half were asked to write about the usefulness of science in their own lives, focusing on its relevance and value. At the end of the semester, the latter group not only reported more interest in science than the former, but also scored an average of a full grade point higher. This result was exceptionally true for those with the lowest probabilities for doing well in class.

Remember that you are an expert with your students and your content. If a strategy is working for your students, you do not have to quit using it, but definitely make sure to use the two high-ranking strategies of practice testing and distributed practice, which are also recommended by Medina (2014) and Küpper-Tetzel, Kapler, and Wiseheart (2014).

Mental Note: Homework provides multiple rehearsals and raises student achievement.

Higher-Level Thinking and Rehearsal

The cognitive process dimension of the revised version of Bloom's taxonomy (Anderson et al., 2001) describes the higher-level thinking skills as *analyzing, evaluating, and creating*. These are the levels we strive for in teaching. They can be addressed during the Rehearsal step in the memory-building process as well as during the Review and Retrieve steps.

When we rehearse, we begin by aiming for the cognitive processes of remembering, understanding, and applying. Remembering encompasses recognition and recall. These are lower levels of thinking, but nonetheless important. To analyze, evaluate, or create, students must have some information to work with. Therefore, it may be important to begin the rehearsal process with simple recall and recognition tasks for the students. As the relevant neural connections strengthen, students will be able to move to the next level and apply the new information. Anderson and colleagues (2001) categorize this step as *executing and implementing*. If procedural knowledge is being learned, this is a crucial step in acquiring a complete understanding and being able to transfer the information. Rehearsal of procedural knowledge may include the application of the procedure to a task with which the student is familiar. Consider the following example.

Mr. Bellows had been working with his students on the scientific method. To reach them, he had several large bowls of popcorn on his desk when the students entered his class on the first day of the unit. The kernels had been recently popped, so the aroma in the room was strong. When the kids asked if they could have some, he explained that they had to first use the scientific method to determine which of the bowls had the fluffiest, tastiest popcorn. He explained the contents of each bowl: popcorn made from homegrown corn, popcorn from a movie theater, and popcorn from a grocery store. The students came to order quickly, knowing that the sooner they figured out the problem, the sooner they could eat!

For reflection, Mr. Bellows asked the students to write in their journals about a popcorn experience that they'd had. He shared his own experience of burning his hand badly with oil once as he poured some popcorn out of a pot. Many of the students had never heard of popping popcorn the old-fashioned way. After the stu-

dents wrote their reflections, Mr. Bellows presented the steps to the scientific method on the whiteboard. The students then had to find a partner and explain those steps before recoding them in their own terms. At that point, Mr. Bellows cruised the classroom, offering reinforcement and suggestions.

The students formalized Mr. Bellows's question and created a hypothesis: "I believe that movie theater popcorn will be the fluffiest and tastiest." They then listed their materials: the types of popcorn, the popper, the oil, and so forth. They wrote down and analyzed every step of the preparation process for each type of popcorn. They recorded their results and observations. Mr. Bellows requested that they add a reflection section to their conclusions.

It was only once Mr. Bellows was certain that the students understood the scientific method and had a written recoding of the steps, as well as the popcorn example, that he assigned homework: to determine which television channel showed the most commercials.

Through this rehearsal and many others, Mr. Bellows attempted to elaborate on the scientific method and repeat it using relevant and meaningful assignments. When his students encounter an unfamiliar problem, such as on the state assessment, they are much more likely to employ the scientific method correctly from their numerous rehearsals.

Analyzing

This level of the cognitive process dimension of the revised Bloom's taxonomy includes differentiating, organizing, and attributing. *Differentiating* involves separating information into relevant and irrelevant parts and then using only the former. For example, in Mr. Bellows's class, students would be analyzing when they read a text and applied the scientific method to its relevant portions. *Organizing* involves identifying the component parts of a situation or problem and how they interact. Mr. Bellows's students would take research reports and organize their analysis according to the steps of the scientific method: hypothesis, method, results, and conclusion. *Attributing* involves deconstructing information and checking for values or bias. Using the scientific method, Mr. Bellows's students would be able to look at the components and analyze the values or find biases of the authors in the method. They would cross-check information and look at sources. Differentiating, organizing, and attributing in this way are all possible homework and practice rehearsals for these students.

Evaluating

Using this higher-level thinking skill involves checking and critiquing. Mr. Bellows could have his students examine research reports that used the scientific method and check for inconsistencies. Perhaps the conclusion is not supported by the data, or the hypothesis is not a clear result of the research question. The students could then continue by critiquing the reports, noting whether the hypotheses are reasonable or recognizing the positive and negative features of the sample.

Creating

Taking students to this level of thinking involves moving from the ordinary to the unique. Considered the highest level of thinking, creating allows students to plan and produce steps and methods to use in unanticipated situations. For example, Mr. Bellows's students may generate their own problems to be solved using the scientific method, plan a lesson to teach the scientific method, or construct their own steps to solving problems that do not meet the standard criteria for the scientific method.

Mental Note: For transfer of learning to occur, students must be able to take their knowledge and understanding and use them when confronted with situations and problems that are unexpected or unusual.

Rehearsal and Multiple Memory Pathways: Many Trips Down Memory's Lanes

A working knowledge of the memory pathways will help identify different rehearsal strategies (see Figure 5.2; see also Fogarty, 2009; Kuczala, 2015; and Lengel & Kuczala, 2010).

FIGURE 5.2	The Five Memory Lanes
Memory Lane	**Strategies**
Semantic	Graphic organizers Mind maps Time lines Peer teaching Practice tests
Episodic	Field trips Bulletin boards and posters Decorations Seating arrangements
Emotional	Music Personalization Storytelling Role-play Debate
Procedural	Dance Role-play Body peg systems Cheers Movement while learning (walking, marching)
Conditioned Response (Automatic)	Songs Poems Flash cards Quiz shows

Semantic instruction is what we do most in school—helping students to take semantic information and make permanent connections to it. However, the semantic memory pathway is only one of the many pathways to learning that we have in our brains:

- The *episodic* pathway stores event and location memories. Students remember guest speakers, new bulletin boards, field trips, and anything else you use to "set the stage" for learning.
- The *emotional* pathway, the strongest pathway we have, stores our memories for emotional events. According to Cahill (2004), the amygdala, the primitive emotional structure in the limbic area of the brain, most affects what we remember. Its many connections throughout the brain allow it to communicate immediately whenever something is important emotionally to remember. Any time you add emotion to these rehearsals, you exponentially enhance memory. Tell stories and use humor in your teaching to include this pathway. As author Karyn Buxman says, "Logic tells; emotion sells!" Get buy-in to your content through your students' emotions.
- The *procedural* pathway is used for muscle memories and basic procedures that we practice repeatedly until they become second nature. The physical movement ideas in this chapter can assist you with this pathway.
- Finally, we can condition certain memories through the *conditioned-response* or *automatic* pathway. Our decoding skills and multiplication tables are stored here, as is other information that is hard to connect to prior experiences.

Through the rehearsal process, we can take information and store it in many or all of these pathways (for more, see Appendix A).

Pathways—or memory lanes, as we might call them—provide multiple possibilities for creating varied experiences for students. For learning to be transferable, we want students to use as many pathways as possible. Of course, they're likely to eventually need to convey their learning using traditional paper-and-pencil tests, so be sure that they are transferring their knowledge to the semantic pathway in writing. By applying what they learn to various contexts, students create a more flexible representation of knowledge (Kihlstrom, 2011).

We must remember that memory is a somewhat developmental process. Anderson and colleagues (2001) note that recall and recognition are lower-level skills. According to DeFina (2003), younger children have difficulty conceptualizing complicated curricula. By the age of 7 or 8, students have the ability to retrieve only one item when using a memory cue, but by 10 or 11, that same cue may help them retrieve three different items. Recall improves as the students get older. For instance, 80 percent of 5th graders can use categories to organize information and help with retrieval. As students progress further through school, they develop the ability to organize information using conceptual categories. Clearly, the types of rehearsal we use with students will vary according to grade level and ability.

Benjamin (2010) tells us that all humans think in stories. The episodes and events of our lives are our stories. By creating lessons that are unique events in the lives of our students, we can assist with their long-term retention. Making rehearsal an event-filled process will secure knowledge in the episodic pathway and eventually in the semantic pathway (Eichenbaum & Dickerson, 2010). Adding emotion to rehearsal strategies is also helpful (e.g., through debates, role-plays, persuasive writing, interviews, and campaigns).

What About Mnemonics?

Hattie and Yates (2014) cite research showing that teachers who teach memory skills create enduring benefits for their students well past the school year. This holds especially true for students who have difficulty with basic skills. Familiar mnemonic techniques for enhancing memory include peg systems, acronyms, acrostics, the method of loci, chaining, and music and rhythm (see Figure 5.3). Many of these help create visual pictures in our minds.

Mnemonics are based on linking what needs to be learned with what is already known, placing information in multiple pathways, adding attention and interest to what is being taught, and storing with cues to make information easier to find. The less prior knowledge a student has, the more helpful mnemonics can be. They take an unusual association and make it memorable.

FIGURE 5.3	Mnemonic Devices to Aid Memory
Mnemonic	**Example/Explanation**
Rhyming Peg System 	Remembering ordered or unordered items by first memorizing a list of keywords that rhyme with a sequence of digits: • One is bun. • Six is bricks. • Two is shoe. • Seven is heaven. • Three is tree. • Eight is gate. • Four is door. • Nine is line. • Five is hive. • Ten is hen.
Acronyms 	A word or phrase made entirely of letters that are cues to words we must remember (e.g., *HOMES* for the Great Lakes: Huron, Ontario, Michigan, Erie, and Superior).
Acrostics 	A sentence in which the first letter of each word is a cue. For example, "A Rat In The House Might Eat The Ice Cream"; the first letters spell *arithmetic*.
Method of Loci 	Using a place and the objects in it to associate with a list of items. Choose a starting place, and as you go around the room, place the item with the object (e.g., bedroom: dresser is for first item, bed for second, lamp for third, picture for fourth, window for fifth).
Chaining 	Constructing a story that contains each element of a list. For example: items to be remembered are counties in the south of England: Avon, Dorset, Somerset, Cornwall, Wiltshire, Devon, Gloucestershire, Hampshire, and Surrey. An **Avon** lady came to my **Dor** and **set** down her wares. She said she had **Some more** to **set**, but the **Corn** was growing over the **wall** of her shop. She said that it was making her flowers **Wilt** and she was **shire** (sure) that the **Dev**il was on her trail. She had **Glossy** teeth with bits of **Ham** stuck in them. **Sure** enough, I slammed the door!
Music and Rhythm 	Create a song or rhyme for the information to be remembered. A great example: In the movie *Born Yesterday*, the amendments to the Constitution are sung.

Because they are not meaningful, they can also be easily forgotten, but effective mnemonics are like the lyrics to a catchy song: once you hear the opening melody or first few lines, you find that you recall the whole thing!

I recently did a teaching presentation at the school of a former student who is now an assistant principal near Chicago. As we discussed the usefulness of jingles for remembering vocabulary, my former student offered to sing the preposition song that she had learned in my middle school class. Almost 30 years after creating and learning the song, she sang it flawlessly and received a round of applause from her staff.

The rhyming peg system in Figure 5.3 can be used to show students how memory works. I like to use the system to impress my students with my amazing memory. I ask them to make a list for me to remember. One student becomes the recorder and writes the numbers 1 through 10 on the board. I turn my back to the board as students call out a number and say the name of the item they want on the list. I make them wait between items until I say "OK." This gives me a few seconds to visualize a connection between the item and the peg. For instance, if one is toilet paper, I picture the sunbeams with toilet paper streaming down from them. I may picture each sheet of paper burning, as the sunbeams are so hot. To elaborate, I might picture those burning streams of toilet paper falling to the earth and setting houses on fire. The more elaborate I make the mental image, the easier it will be to remember.

When the list is complete, I dazzle my students by telling them each item in any order they choose. After the applause, I offer to teach them how to do it. The younger the students, the shorter I make the original list. For elementary students, begin with four or five items. First, they must learn the peg system, which could take from a few minutes to a few days. After teaching them the peg words, give them a list of groceries, school supplies, or something else. Remind students to make a connection between each item and each peg. Allow them several minutes to make connections. Remind them that they cannot write anything down; this is a visual process that takes their brains' memory power. When all is said and done, students are bound to be amazed at themselves.

Although mnemonics are effective for recalling factual information, conceptual understanding requires more meaningful elaborative rehearsal. If you expect your students to use memory strategies, you must teach them how to use them. Many strategies are second nature to us now that we are adults, but we were not born with them—they were taught to us. As with any other type of memory, we need to rehearse the rehearsal strategies to get them into long-term memory and have them at our disposal when we need them.

☀ **Mental Note: Mnemonics are made as a memory aid.**

Mental and Physical Rehearsal

We have all read studies of how athletes and musicians mentally rehearse the plays in their playbooks or their musical selections. In the same way, we can practice any type of information. A single mental run-through can be valuable; several are even better. Mental practice involves visualization, and visualization is a crucial component of rehearsal and long-term memory. When students are taking tests, they must call upon their visualization abilities to enhance memory. According to Marsh (2013), "If you visualize what you hear, you can visualize what you read." As we demonstrate, dramatize, tell stories, or explain in the classroom, our students can visualize the actual moment when their understanding began. In science, you might say to students, "I want you to take a moment and replay in your minds how you worked the experiment." In math, we might say, "Imagine in your minds the two trains heading out of the stations from their locations. One is traveling more rapidly than the other. . . ." Authors of fiction generally paint us a picture with their words, but informational text may require more effort to picture what the author is trying to communicate. Graphic organizers can enhance the visualization process in these situations. According to Tileston and Darling (2009), when students use graphic representations to show visual patterns, achievement can go up by as much as 49 percentile points!

Movement is also known to enhance learning by adding another pathway for storage, heightening energy levels, and increasing blood flow to the brain.

The most effective physical rehearsals connect to both the semantic and procedural pathways. In social studies, have students dress as historical figures or act out an important event. In math, students can stand and use their arms to demonstrate different types of angles. In science, assign students different steps of the scientific method and give them 30 seconds to physically arrange themselves in the correct order. In English, have students act out a scene from a story. Homework and practice should also offer students opportunities to move their bodies.

Sample Lesson from 3rd Grade Math

Standard: Students should develop understanding of fractions as parts of unit wholes, as parts of a collection, and as divisions of whole numbers.

Reach: *As math time began, Mr. Rogers asked for a volunteer. Germil raised his hand and was chosen. Mr. Rogers took out a long piece of red yarn. He asked the students, "If I wanted to tie this yarn around Germil to divide him into two halves, where would I tie it?" The students suggested at the waist, so Mr. Rogers tied it there. "Now what if I wanted to show you one-fourth of him?" The students chose a spot around his shoulders. Mr. Rogers then took out a piece of yarn for each student, and they spent several minutes putting the yarn in various spots to indicate fractions of Germil.*

Reflect: *Mr. Rogers asked the students to use a PMI chart for reflection. They wrote what they thought were the pluses of using fractions, then the minuses, and finally what was interesting about them. The students took some time completing their charts as they made connections with prior knowledge.*

Recode: *Mr. Rogers had the students write a list of times in their lives when knowing fractions came in helpful. Most students described such experiences as sharing a candy bar with a friend, baking a cake, or dividing money from a lemonade stand.*

Reinforce: *Mr. Rogers cruised the room, checking what each student wrote. He cleared up a few misconceptions and gave positive reinforcement to his students.*

Rehearse: *Mr. Rogers knew that students would need many rehearsals to truly learn fractions, and he wanted to be sure to move the students to some higher-level thinking. (The rehearsals and positive attributes of each are presented in*

Figure 5.4.) He included a reflection or reinforcement step after each rehearsal, too. The students seemed to understand well.

FIGURE 5.4	Rehearsals for Understanding Fractions	
Rehearsal		Memory Enhancers
1. Mr. Rogers brought in small containers of Play-Doh. Students picked three different colors. Then he asked them to pick the first color and remove one-fourth, pick the second color and remove one-third, and take one-half from the final color.		Movement, manipulatives
2. For the second rehearsal, the class used the Play-Doh activity again; however, after removing the fractional amounts, the students discussed the fraction that was left inside the container.		Movement, manipulatives, reasoning
3. The third rehearsal was making a poster of the students' favorite fraction. They wrote their fraction and then drew examples of items that could be cut to get that fraction (e.g., pies, apples, oranges, candy bars).		Movement, drawing, exemplifying
4. Mr. Rogers brought in the "pies" from the game Trivial Pursuit. He had enough for each student. The pies contained six equal triangles. The students discovered that six-sixths was a whole pie. Then they removed one-third of the pie and talked about the fact that they removed two one-sixth portions and so forth.		Movement, manipulatives, understanding
5. The students walked through the building in pairs to find items that are fractions. For instance, some found a glass of water that was half full, pencils that had been sharpened down to a third of their usual size, and trash cans that were two-thirds full.		Movement, collaboration, real world, understanding
6. Mr. Rogers brought in two whole pizzas. There were 22 students in the class and, with their teacher, they needed to cut the pizzas to make 23 slices. The students figured out that the fairest way to slice the pizzas was into 12 equal slices for each pizza. The extra slice was given to the principal.		Hands-on, multisensory, real world, understanding

Rehearsal	Memory Enhancers
7. As the students were able to apply their knowledge, Mr. Rogers wanted to see if they could work backward by analyzing how much sand was in a bowl. Using the larger spoon first, each pair was to determine how many teaspoons and fractions of teaspoons were in the bowl.	Hands-on, collaboration, analysis, evaluation
8. Mr. Rogers brought in a bag of candy for each group of four students. They were to separate the candy by colors. They counted the total number of candies and figured what fraction of the total each color represented. These were snack-size bags, so the number in each was limited.	Collaboration, hands-on, evaluation, analysis, application
9. The students used round circles of colored construction paper. They were to divide the first in half, the second in thirds, the third in fourths, and so forth.	Manipulatives, evaluation, analysis, application
10. The students were given a diagram of a huge ice cream sundae, with 60 scoops in the bowl. Mr. Rogers asked, "If they color 30 scoops chocolate, 20 scoops strawberry, and 10 scoops vanilla, what is the fraction of the whole sundae that each flavor represents?"	Hands-on, deduction, analysis, synthesis, application
11. The students were asked to create their own ice cream sundae and choose the flavors for each scoop. Then they determined the fractional part of the whole sundae each flavor represented.	Creativity, evaluation, analysis, application

From Working Memory to Long-Term Retention

The purpose of rehearsal is to expand connections for conceptual, procedural, and factual knowledge. By spacing out opportunities to rehearse using multiple memory pathways, students have the opportunity to catch up on sleep to enhance memory storage. Rehearsal allows permanent changes to take place in the brain, solidifying neural connections to aid transfer. If information can be stored in all of the memory pathways, then it can be accessed easily through various memory cues.

Reflection

1. Rehearsal is the ideal time to reach all students through their individual learning preferences. Homework and practice can be offered in different modalities.

2. Learning in small increments with practice in between is a more accurate way of storing information.

3. Consider each practice or rehearsal an episode. Take into account the environment in which you are teaching. Making your instruction unique through posters, pictures, and varied room arrangements may help with storage and retrieval of information.

4. Encourage students to implement their own rehearsals. Rehearsing new material each night before bedtime for just a few minutes can increase retention.

Review

Cramming seeks to stamp things in by intense application immediately before the ordeal. But a thing thus learned can form but few associations.

—*William James*

It was the day before the test on insects. My friend and colleague, Laurel, looked at her lesson-plan book. Across the top of the page, in bold letters, was the word REVIEW.

I have been so busy with all of these insect activities that I haven't even looked at the assessment, *she thought.* Our school has a brand-new textbook series, and the publisher has provided assessments.

Laurel walked over to the filing cabinet and pulled out the "Insect" folder. She found several worksheets that she didn't bother using. She'd been teaching the unit for years and had enough material to keep her students busy learning all day long. She grabbed the sheet that said "Post-assessment." The title startled her—it means there must have been a pre-assessment, and she doesn't think she used that. Oh, well, *she tells herself,* I'll just look this over and make sure I covered everything.

Much to her dismay, Laurel realized that the publisher's test not only covered material that she hadn't, but also left out some information that she thought was important. She dug deeper into her cabinet to find the assessment she had given her 3rd graders last year. In comparing the two, she decided the publisher's test better addressed the material. Now what? She looked at her schedule and thought about her plans after school. Did she have the time and energy to create a new assessment? Should she delay the test? The answer to each question was no. She was attending a workshop in two days and didn't want a substitute to give the test.

Laurel decided to teach the material on the test that she hadn't covered during her review. After all, this information was in the text that the students were supposed to have read.

You can guess the results. This is something we probably all have done at some time in our careers—before we understood more about the brain and how kids learn and remember. This was review: a session a day or two before the test when either the teacher went over what was on the assessment, or the teacher asked the students if they had any questions on the material. Especially at the middle and high school levels, I was always amazed at the short review sessions I had—and then I was disappointed at the test scores. It didn't take too long until I learned an important fact: Kids don't know what they don't know. So, asking them for their questions was a total waste of time. The only students who would come up with a question were the ones who knew the material well enough to ask about a particular nuance.

☀ **Mental Note: Kids don't know what they don't know.**

Why Review?

Schacter (2001) describes three "sins" of memory—blocking, misattribution, and transience—that the Review step can help allay.

Blocking occurs when information is stored but cannot be accessed. We've all had the experience of seeing a former student and being unable to recall her name. This is sometimes called the "tip of the tongue" phenomenon: We know the name and just can't quite spit it out. Yet a short while later, the name inevitably comes to us. A similar thing happens to our students in the classroom: They know the answer, but in an assessment situation, they can't access it. Blocking often arises with proper nouns: names of people, places, documents, and so on. Common nouns usually have synonyms that can be substituted for them. A student writing about the Vietnam conflict who can't recall the word *combat* can use *battle* or *struggle* instead, but the name of a specific battle or location can't be substituted.

Misattribution, also known as *source memory problems,* is the attribution of a memory to the wrong situation or source and is especially common among students. Until the frontal lobes are fully developed, people often have difficulty discerning their sources of information (Dehn, 2010). Consider the following example.

In class, we were discussing the hypothalamus—the structure below the thalamus that communicates with the pituitary gland and therefore plays a role in controlling body temperature, emotions, hunger, thirst, circadian rhythms, and hormones. It is also responsible for fat metabolism.

On the bus after school, some of my students were discussing their brains. The girls agreed that the hypothalamus regulated their hunger and talked about the types of diet drugs and exercise they used to control weight. One of the boys sitting close by said he read in a fitness magazine that the hippocampus responds by producing new neurons whenever you exercise.

A few days later, I gave my students a practice test on what they'd learned about the brain material—not for a grade, but to allow for more reinforcement and correction through recoding. The practice test also gave them the opportunity to transfer information from other pathways to the semantic pathway. Part of the assessment was multiple choice, and one of the questions was as follows: "The structure most likely to affect and be affected by diet and exercise is (a) the amygdala, (b) the thalamus, (c) the hippocampus, or (d) the hypothalamus."

Most of the students answered that question quickly by marking "(d) the hypothalamus," but two of the girls and one boy involved in that bus conversation answered "(c) the hippocampus." Why? Because they had remembered bits of the conversation about the hippocampus and exercise and confused the source—they thought I had given them that information.

Had I given them a review before the practice test, this problem may not have occurred. We would have reexamined the structures and functions and possibly erased the misconception from their brains. Because the test was only for practice, the analysis of the test answers served as a review and corrected the students' misplaced source information.

Transience, sometimes referred to as *the forgetting curve* or *the fading theory,* refers to a memory being lost over time. This theory suggests that the neural connections in the brain will weaken without use; in other words, "Use it or lose it!" One study of student retention of textbook material (Keeley, 1997) found that

- 54 percent of the material was remembered after 1 day,
- 35 percent of the material was remembered after 7 days,
- 21 percent of the material was remembered after 14 days, and
- 8 percent of the material was remembered after 21 days.

Another study, also cited by Keeley, found that after 14 days, participants forgot *90 percent* of the information they had learned!

According to Schenck (2011), spacing reviews throughout the learning and increasing the time between them gradually allows long-term networks to be strengthened. For both traditional and standardized testing, the timing between repeated reviews can significantly affect how much information students retain. Schenck found that typical test review takes place long after the initial learning and rehearsal. He suggests that we review from the beginning with short intervals in between, then increase the time between reviews (see Figure 6.1).

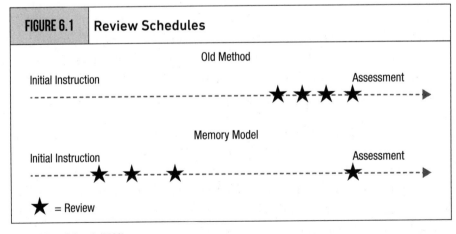

FIGURE 6.1   **Review Schedules**

Old Method

Initial Instruction   Assessment

Memory Model

Initial Instruction   Assessment

★ = Review

Adapted from Schenck (2000).

☀ **Mental Note: Without review, important information may be lost.**

Jane, our science teacher, was covering a unit on volcanoes. Her target was an objective for earth science: to know how landforms are created through a combination of constructive and destructive forces. Constructive forces include crustal deformation, volcanoes, and deposition of sediment; destructive forces include weathering and erosion. Jane's students had created visuals of the vocabulary words, discussed and written about "the year without a summer, 1816," seen video clips of volcanoes, completed a PMI chart, and discussed pictures of Jane's visit to a Hawaiian volcano. Allowing for the interruptions of school assemblies, all of this practice took one week.

Jane's next experience for the students was to take a field trip to the science museum to learn about predicting volcanoes. Before the trip, Jane was to conduct her first review. She wanted to be sure that the students had a conceptual understanding of the material. She had written a selected response test for the unit, so she wanted her reviews to match the assessment. To reach her students, Jane chose a Trivial Pursuit game for review. She hadn't come up with the questions for it; she was going to divide the students into two groups and ask each one to create the questions for the other. Some of the questions the students ended up designing were multiple choice, and others were short answer. Jane was delighted because these formats would closely match her assessment. The students enjoyed both aspects of the review, creating and participating. Jane gave them feedback on the questions they missed that they did not understand.

The day of the trip, Jane handed out a graphic organizer for the students to jot down the steps they would be learning. The day after the trip, when she saw the students again, she had them do a four-corner reflection of the trip and share their organizers in small groups. The following day, Jane had the students break into pairs and conduct online research on a famous volcanic eruption, determine the scientific evidence that was available at the time for predictions, and write about the impact the eruption had on the civilization surrounding it. This project took several days.

Knowing that memory is fragile, Jane planned another review. This time she chose a mind map for the class to create together using colored markers and butcher paper on the bulletin board. They began by writing the word volcanoes *in the middle of the paper and enclosing it in a cloud of "volcanic dust." Jane called only on those who wished to participate and, taking turns, they drew major detail lines, briefly described each detail, and created a symbol for each one. They included subtopics, details, and vocabulary words in the same color below each line. Jane prompted the students using multiple-choice questions to remain aligned with her assessment. They completed the mind map that Jane could now use and add to for her next review.*

The unit continued with problem solving. Jane addressed the temperature of lava—1,150 degrees Celsius—and asked students to translate the temperature into Fahrenheit.

A few weeks later, the unit ended. Jane had three reviews of the material before the final assessment, and her students did very well.

According to Schenck (2011), if students have been actively involved in their learning and review takes place two or three weeks later, the students should retain most of the knowledge for two to three months.

> ☀ **Mental Note: Review can increase the length of time that students remember.**

Procrastination and Cramming

A lack of appropriate reviews leaves students on their own to figure out how they are going to be successful in school and, in particular, on exams. Although most teachers suggest that students look over their notes each night for a few minutes, unfortunately, few really do so. Overlooking the fact that this type of review provides the fodder needed for the brain to practice during sleep, this practice will also afford the number of repetitions necessary to move information securely into long-term memory.

If a student does not follow the advice of reviewing each night, and if the teacher does not offer reviews during class time, we often find that students put off studying until the last minute. This procrastination leads to cramming, as discussed in the previous chapter. This is not a way to remember any information for the long term. Sommer (2010) studied university students who crammed for tests and found the following characteristics: calculated procrastination, preparatory anxiety, climactic cramming, nick-of-time deadline making, and, sometimes, victory (but only if the information is forgotten *after* the assessment, not before!).

Research shows that cramming can indeed raise test scores (Schenck, 2011; Vacha & McBride, 1993). For example, Crew (1969) found that students who crammed for two hours before a test scored considerably higher than those who did not. After the test, however, students who crammed did not retain the knowledge. As each year passed, cramming time grew longer, as there was more and more to review at each successive grade level. With newer standards that call for more essay writing and more complex readings and questions, it has become prudent to teach to whatever standards your state or district is following and skip the last-minute test preparation.

How Do We Review?

Review of factual information may be a matter of reorganization. Remember that we are taking information from long-term memory, bringing it into working memory, examining it to ensure accuracy, and taking an opportunity perhaps to reorganize it to enhance transfer. I have the following goals with any review:

- Match the review to instruction and assessment.
- Check for accuracy of the memory.
- Give students the conditions to use higher-level thinking skills to analyze, evaluate, and possibly create alternative ways to use the knowledge.
- Strengthen the existing networks.
- For high-stakes testing, practice similar questions under similar conditions.
- Eliminate cramming.

ACT (2016/17) recommends the following three strategies for test preparation:

1. Familiarize yourself with the content of the tests.
2. Refresh your knowledge and skills in the content areas.
3. Identify the content areas you have not studied.

If review is done intermittently, as previously suggested, then we may be able to avoid students cramming right before the test. Tuckman (1998) found that learners who procrastinate performed better on final exams if they had received frequent quizzes. These results are similar to those of a study by Wenglinsky (2002), who found that students whose teachers periodically gave them paper-and-pencil tests scored higher on standardized tests.

Pop Quizzes

Having created brain-compatible classrooms for 15 years, I used to dismiss the notion of the pop quiz. After all, an unannounced quiz can cause stress, and I wanted my classroom to be as stress-free as possible.

One summer, though, I changed my mind. I was conducting a five-day workshop based on my 2002 book *Becoming a Wiz at Brain-Based Teaching*. There were 70 participants, including K–12 teachers, specialists, school psychologists, and administrators. When the discussion of stress began, I shared ways of de-stressing the classroom, such as incorporating music and rituals, teaching like a coach, and using clear targets and rubrics. When asked how I felt about pop quizzes, I replied that I no longer used them because I felt they raised students' stress levels too much.

At the break, a high school Spanish teacher approached me looking quite concerned. He said he gave pop quizzes regularly. He liked them because the kids did their assignments and practiced to keep up their grades. He was wondering if he should change his whole approach. We decided we would both do some research before the end of the week and discuss it.

I was surprised at the research I found. Learning by taking practice tests, a strategy known as *retrieval practice,* can protect memory against the negative effects of stress, according to researchers at Tufts University (Smith,

Floerke, & Thomas, 2016). Participants were asked to learn a set of 30 words with 30 images. These were introduced through a computer program, which displayed one item at a time for a few seconds each. Participants were allowed 10 seconds after each to take notes. One group of participants then studied using retrieval practice, and took timed practice tests in which they freely recalled as many items as they could remember. The other group used study practice. For these participants, information was displayed on a computer screen. Participants were given multiple timed periods to study. The retrieval practice group did better than the study practice group.

The Tufts study is similar to the one I refer to in *101 Strategies to Make Academic Vocabulary Stick,* in which students review simply by writing everything they know on a blank sheet:

> In a study by Szpunar, Chan, and McDermott (2009), three groups of students learned a set of words on computers in five sessions with a 20-minute break between each session. During the breaks, members of group A spent the time as they pleased; members of group B stayed at the computer and went over the words and definitions they had just learned; and members of group C received a blank sheet of paper and were asked to write down everything they remembered from the session. On the unit tests and the final test, group C outscored both of the other groups by about 40 percent. Interestingly, group B did not do much better than group A. This study shows why it is imperative not only to motivate students to attend to the instructional portion of a lesson but also to teach them how to recode and internalize the new information once the lesson is over. (Sprenger, 2017, p. 14)

If quizzes are given often enough, I believe that they can become part of the class ritual. Therefore, expecting those quizzes and preparing for them may have relieved some of the students' stress in the above studies, as well as in the Spanish teacher's class.

> ☀ **Mental Note: Quizzes as review may increase test scores on subsequent examinations.**

Reviewing According to Marzano

Reviewing content is one of the elements discussed in Marzano's *The New Art and Science of Teaching* (2017). The book covers the following eight specific reviewing strategies: *cumulative review, cloze activity, summary, presented problem, demonstration, brief practice test or exercise, questioning,* and *give one, get one.*

1. **Cumulative review:** Students review content from the current unit and relate it to previous units. This strategy is similar to one in which a mind map is created at the beginning of the year and every unit covered is mapped. As each unit is completed and mapped, the teacher makes time to discuss connections from the most recently completed unit to each of the previous units. Granted, this may be easier in some subject areas, such as history, than others, but I have seen the strategy used successfully in math and science, as well.

2. **Cloze activity:** Sentences with missing words or phrases are presented to the students. The missing information is from the unit that is being completed. This is a great activity as an introduction to new learning, as well. Students like cloze activities. You can provide a word or phrase bank, but usually at the end of a unit, students are expected to know the information and recall it from memory.

3. **Summary:** The teacher has the class write short reviews of the material or provides them with reviews to discuss. Remember that a summary at the end of a unit used for review is simply a tool for recall.

4. **Presented problem:** The teacher presents a problem for the students to solve using previously learned material. Applying learned information in a new and unanticipated situation is the essence of what we want our students to be able to do.

5. **Demonstration:** The teacher asks students to demonstrate a skill or process that they have learned—if they can teach it, they know it.

6. **Brief practice test or exercise:** The teacher provides a practice test that prompts students to remember and apply information they've previously learned. After the test, students may ask questions about any information they don't understand.

7. **Questioning:** The teacher asks questions that require students to recall, recognize, or apply previously learned information. Although we ultimately want our students asking questions, most teachers are keenly aware that students don't know what they don't know and therefore have difficulty doing so.

8. **Give one, get one:** Students write information on a specific topic in their notebooks, break into pairs, and compare what they wrote with what their partner wrote. You may want to have students take a sheet of paper and fold it in half, hot-dog style. Ask students to write "Give one" at the top of the left column and "Get one" on the right. Then provide information or a question such as, "What are the reasons for the Vietnam conflict?" Students write their reasons briefly in the left-hand column. Then they walk around and find a partner. One student begins by sharing his list. When the other student hears something that she hasn't written, she writes it down. Now it is the second student's turn to go down her list for the other student. Students repeat the process until the time is up.

Other Ways to Review

Factual information may be reviewed differently than conceptual information. For things such as formulas, definitions, or lists of information, students may want to make flashcards, set the information to music or a chant, or review using rote repetition. Each of these methods will access different memory pathways described in Chapter 5.

Conceptual information needs to be more comprehensively reviewed. Mind mapping is one of my favorite review tools (see Figure 6.2 for a mind map on how to create a mind map). I arrange my students in teams for this activity. On the review day, I have a 12-by-8-inch sheet of construction paper for each group. Students get out their markers, and I ask them to create a mind map of the concepts that we are covering. If we are using a text, they may use that, their notes, and any of the recoding and rehearsal materials they have. In groups, students usually finish this task in 20 or 30 minutes. We then put the maps up on a wall or bulletin board for all to see. The students examine each other's maps and may add to their own if they see that it is missing important information.

As I said earlier, my students don't know what they don't know—but after this activity, they do. This is when they ask questions and I provide them with feedback and reinforcement.

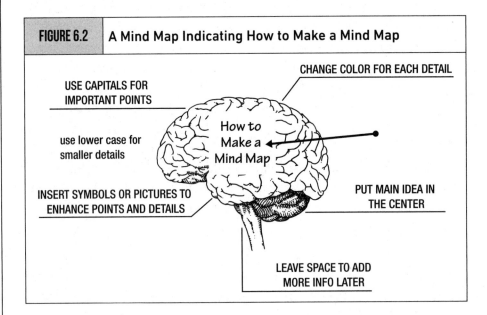

FIGURE 6.2   A Mind Map Indicating How to Make a Mind Map

Other reviewing strategies include webs, concept maps, notes, and checklists. Try to create the same environment for review as the students will face during testing. If the assessment has open-ended questions, so should the review. If recognition memory is going to be employed, make recognizing answers part of the review. Take this opportunity to apply the material to the real world. You probably did this through some of the rehearsal strategies you used, but offering a problem or situation that is relevant to the students and follows the same game plan as previous rehearsals will be helpful. Be sure to refer to the rehearsals that you have used. This will spark some memories as well as provide practice.

If the assessment is paper-and-pencil, you might need to help students transfer knowledge to the semantic pathway. For instance, if they spent most of their rehearsals using math manipulatives, but you are going to give them a written test with problems to solve, you need to spend time helping them transfer what they learned to paper. You can assist this process by reminding students what they did with the manipulatives. Perhaps they can visualize the process and practice applying it on paper. The difficulty some students have transferring process and product to paper creates achievement gaps. If I asked you to tell me how to tie a shoe without using your hands or looking at your feet, you would be able to do it, but with some difficulty or discomfort. You would have to use some brainpower to transfer this information that is conveniently stored in your procedural pathway to the semantic pathway to explain the process. With practice you could do so quickly and easily, but in the beginning it takes time and effort. So it is with our students who are trying to transfer. Any emotional connections that your students may have to the learning should be included in the review. If you reached your students through the emotional pathway when you introduced the knowledge, remind them of it during the review. Any emotional moments throughout the lessons or unit when there was laughter, excitement, or sadness may trigger memories. Every time we recall something, we are rehearsing or reviewing it. The review step is the chance to let your students "call up" the memories that they will need for the assessment—or for life!

Mental Note: Emotions that were engaged during instruction and rehearsal should be engaged during review.

Review, Transfer, and Higher-Level Thinking

From the Rehearse step, our students should have plenty of conceptual information, as well as simple facts, stored in long-term memory. The review, then, may be a time for climbing the new taxonomy by analyzing, evaluating, and creating. You may ask your students to take their new long-term understandings and separate relevant from irrelevant material. Perhaps they can take themes, morals, or lessons learned and apply them to their own lives. When studying *Julius Caesar,* for instance, students analyze Brutus and Cassius while comparing them to present-day individuals. During a review on consumerism, students create commercials that show their conceptual understanding of media influences. Perhaps, in a social science review, students evaluate individual battles and their contributions to the war effort.

Sample Unit from 7th Grade English

Mrs. Fox had followed her plans carefully. Using a backward design model, she began with what she wanted the students to know. She then developed an assessment that would let them show her that they had learned, retained, and could transfer information. She was certain her students had long-term storage for her unit on the novel The Giver *by Lois Lowry. She had more than one recoding session, because she wanted her students to consider several themes. Her unit design looked like this:*

Reach #1: When the students entered the classroom on the first day of the unit, they had to choose whether to sit on the side of the room labeled "Here" or on the side labeled "Elsewhere." They were not allowed to ask questions until all were seated. They brainstormed ideas about the differences between Here and Elsewhere, then began reading the book.

Reflection #1: The students were asked to write in their journals about how they felt about the unknown. What if they were leaving to go Elsewhere?

Reach #2: On the second day, students entered the room to find the song "Memories" playing. Mrs. Fox asked them to think of their favorite memories and share them with others.

Reflection #2: *Students labeled a page in their journal "Memories." They wrote as many important memories as they could in five minutes, then continued reading.*

Recode: *The students wrote examples of the importance of memory and survival in* The Giver. *They compared and contrasted a life without memory and pain to a life with both.*

Reinforce: *Through Socratic questioning, Mrs. Fox cleared up any misunderstandings the students had, writing their input on the board and promising to consider all of it.*

Rehearsal #1: *To get information into the procedural memory pathway, students role-played several scenes from the novel.*

Reflection #3: *After the role-play, the students discussed the activity, especially how they felt it went. This process helps strengthen memory.*

Rehearsal #2: *After discussing the definitions of similes and metaphors, students wrote three of their own using the story characters Gabriel and Jonas and the concept of release.*

Reflection #4: *Mrs. Fox asked the students to write some of their favorite metaphors in their journals and offer a short explanation to help understand and remember them.*

Rehearsal #3: *The students compared and contrasted our society to the society in the novel.*

Reflection #5: *Mrs. Fox asked students to address the following question in their journals: "Which society do you think is better? Are there any aspects of Jonas's society that you would like ours to adopt?"*

Rehearsal #4: *Students made posters of their world in black and white, hung them up on the walls, and talked in groups about the importance of color.*

Reflection #6: *Mrs. Fox asked students to take some time to imagine their world in black and white, with no color ever. What effect did they think this would have on them and their families?*

Rehearsal #5: *Students rewrote* The Giver *as a news article. This exercise ensured that the basic facts of the story were clear in their minds.*

Reflection #7: *The students reflected on their article's tone and whether it matched the tone of the original story.*

Review: After providing students with feedback regarding the accuracy of their news articles, Mrs. Fox asked them to exchange their articles with each other and write an editorial based on the one they received. Mrs. Fox then provided the students with feedback on their editorials.

Rehearsal #6: Having completed a Holocaust unit earlier in the year, Mrs. Fox asked the students to compare and contrast extinction efforts in history. They brought in information from the previous unit and made text-to-text and text-to-world connections.

Reflection #8: Because the Holocaust is a sensitive topic, Mrs. Fox provided students with the opportunity to write about their feelings in their journals.

Rehearsal #7: To offer analysis, evaluation, and creativity, the students were asked to compose either a prequel or a sequel of The Giver.

Reflection #9: Mrs. Fox asked the students to write a brief paragraph explaining how their prequels or sequels added to the original story.

Rehearsal #8: Students conducted online research on one of the following topics: daycare, surrogate mothers, euthanasia, or volunteerism.

The rehearsals in this unit took several class periods and required homework in most cases. Mrs. Fox had students discuss each project in small or large groups. After the eight rehearsals and the review, Mrs. Fox decided to test her students' long-term memory. A paper-and-pencil assessment in the form of a practice quiz with the following recall questions gave her some of the information she was seeking:

- In *The Giver,* is everyone equal? Is everyone the same? Explain the difference between equal and the same.
- The concept of release is important in Jonas's community. What are the advantages of this concept? Are there disadvantages? What specific examples can provide proof for your answers?
- Compare our society to Jonas's. What are the advantages of each?
- Differences between men and women are different in Jonas's society than in ours. What customs do they have to distinguish differences between the two?

When some students did poorly on the assessment, Mrs. Fox checked to see whether their performance indicated a storage problem or a retrieval problem. To do this, she offered them a recognition test consisting of matching, true/false, and multiple-choice questions such as the following example:

Place an E next to the statements that are examples of being equal and an S next to the statements that are examples of being the same.

___*A. All jobs are not equally respected. (Ex.: Mother tells Lily Birthmothers are not respected; the job of Receiver obviously carries more honor than others.)*

___*B. In the Ceremonies, everyone gets the same things (haircuts, calculators, bikes, clothing, comfort objects, names, parents, birthdays) at the same age and time.*

___*C. The rules and laws apply equally to everyone.*

___*D. Release of everyone who is different, unhealthy, old, or who disagrees means everyone is basically the same.*

___*E. Apologies and politeness are extended to everyone of all ages.*

___*F. Everyday routines (dream sharing, feeling sharing, etc.) are the same for everyone.*

___*G. No rich or poor, no poverty in the Community—everyone is paid the same (nothing, because there is no money).*

This and other recognition questions revealed a great deal. The students who didn't do well on the recall test and performed better on the recognition test were having a retrieval problem. The information was stored, because they could recognize it when they saw it. For these students, Mrs. Fox found activities that helped them access the information. By contrast, students who did not do well on the recognition test had a storage problem (Mason & Kohn, 2001). The information was not in their long-term memory. This could've been due to inattentiveness or lack of sleep, or the students may just have needed more time and more rehearsals.

Mental Note: If students can't recall or recognize, it's a storage problem. If they can recognize but not recall, it's a retrieval problem.

Reteaching

Review may show us that our students were unable to store information in long-term memory or that it is difficult for them to retrieve. In such cases, reteaching is important. Crowley and Siegler (1999) found that comprehension increases when students first receive a visual demonstration of new learning. Then a verbal explanation follows from someone else. Finally, the recoding strategy is implemented—a reiteration of the material in the learner's own words. Even though you started out in this way when you followed the steps for memory building, this shortened version makes more sense at this point in the process. Because some of your students will not need the reteaching component, perhaps they can be the teachers. This exercise will reinforce their learning, as it provides new and varied experiences for learners in need.

Teaching in the Fast Lane (2017) offers the following six strategies and recommendations for reteaching:

1. **Building Schema:** This strategy addresses the fact that many of our students lack the necessary prior knowledge. Consider using YouTube videos to fill in these gaps.

2. **Peer Coaching:** Sometimes students have heard enough from us and need a peer to explain it. Instead of asking the class star on the subject, ask a student who is just starting to understand the material.

3. **Cooperative Learning:** Use the "Sage and Scribe" technique, in which one student speaks and the other writes down what the first student says before switching roles. It works well and encourages students to use academic vocabulary while speaking.

4. **Focusing on Vocabulary:** Use the "Photo Quick Writes" technique, in which the teacher provides students with a photo to write about and a word bank for them to use for the purpose.

5. **Using Visuals:** Mind maps, anchor charts, and other visuals help students relearn.

6. **Checking for Understanding Often:** This strategy helps us see if the students have missed any important connections in the learning.

※ **Mental Note: Reteaching should be a productive experience for all.**

Review of Test-Taking Strategies

I once heard a speaker say that teachers attempt "assumicide" by assuming that our students have prior knowledge when they don't. We assume that they have memory strategies. We assume that they understand. And we assume that they know how to take a test. Research suggests otherwise. One study of 4th graders found an increase in achievement of 19 percent for those taught test-taking strategies every year (Harris, 2014). More sizeable gains were shown in two other studies on students in upper grades (Carter et al., 2005; Holzer, Madaus, Bray, & Kehle, 2009). Even just writing about one's worries before a high-stakes exam can boost test scores by more than 10 percent (Ramirez & Beilock, 2011).

Teaching the critical vocabulary of your standards, goals, or outcomes is vital if students are to do well on their tests. Upon examining both state and national standards, I found 55 high-frequency words (Sprenger, 2013). The research is clear about vocabulary: 85 percent of our students' test scores are based on their knowledge of the vocabulary of their standards (Marzano & Kendall, 1996). If you are preparing students for state or national testing, be sure that you know what the vocabulary requirements are for your grade level (and the grade levels below you). For instance, the word *analyze* is generally introduced at the 5th grade level in most standards. Prior to that grade, students will not need to know the verb. Most verbs in the standards reflect process skills, and if students don't know how to perform such skills, they will not know how to answer the questions. For my list of words, see my book *Teaching the Critical Vocabulary of the Common Core* (Sprenger, 2013). Vocabulary.com offers a useful list of tiered words used on the Smarter Balanced Assessments at www.vocabulary.com/lists/932902. Better yet, go through your standards with your colleagues and pick out the words your students will need to know. Take a look at tests from previous years that have been released and check out the vocabulary used in their questions. Knowing these words will make a difference for your students and their scores.

Here are some other test-taking issues to review:

- If the font or print size on the test is going to be different from what your students are accustomed to, use that font and print size for the reviews.
- If the test is going to be timed, review and practice using that same time limit.
- If the seating must be in a special pattern, have your students sit in that pattern for several days prior to the test.
- If the students are accustomed to having music in the background when they take classroom assessments but music is not allowed on the standardized test, give them practice tests without music.
- If some of your students are sound-sensitive, suggest that everyone (even teachers) wear soft-soled shoes or sneakers the day of the assessment.

 Mental Note: Provide instruction in study skills, such as paraphrasing, outlining, guided note taking, developing cognitive maps, and using advance organizers.

Retrieving, Reworking, and Re-Storing Memories

Review encourages our students to retrieve memories from long-term storage areas. It provides more practice in accessing memories and manipulating them in new ways in working memory. Every time we access a memory, we are more likely to be able to access it again. We can continue to call on higher levels of thinking by asking students to recall conceptual understandings and apply them in different situations.

If we are preparing students for standardized testing, we are teaching them the essentials of certain goals, standards, and benchmarks. The test-makers will determine how our students will show what they know.

Because we have little control over this, the more wide-ranging rehearsals and reviews we provide, the better, and we should always conduct some review under the same circumstances as the assessments will be delivered. Multiple coding will make access to long-term memories easier (Squire & Kandel, 2008).

Teaching to create accessible memories is a continual process of storage, retrieval, and storing again. As we vary our rehearsals and reviews, we provide new "storerooms" for our memories.

Reflection

1. When you plan your unit, plan your reviews. Space them in the manner suggested in Figure 6.1.
2. Some factual information may require rote memorization. If your students have trouble with facts, recommend the mnemonics from Chapter 5.
3. Though reviews may seem to eat up a lot of our time, adequately spaced reviewing may actually save time in the long run.
4. How can you increase the frequency of review in your class?

Retrieve

When we encode a memory, the hippocampus creates a snapshot of the sensory information and files it away. When a memory is encoded and stored correctly, it is readily retrievable.

—*Daniel Schacter*

You are driving to work (implicit procedural memory). The bell is ringing as you arrive, so you jump out of the car and dash into the building (implicit stimulus response). You enter your classroom, switch on the lights, boot up the computer, and turn on the music (implicit procedural memory). Two students dash in and tell you they have to help in the office for a few minutes, so would you please order hot lunch for them? You repeat their names and their lunch requests over and over (immediate semantic memory). The other students are seated, and you look over the class to take attendance. There is an empty seat. You close your eyes to picture who sits there (explicit episodic memory). Aha! It's Charles. You remember that Charles told you he had a dental appointment today (explicit, semantic), which reminds you of your last trip to the dentist for your root canal. You cringe at the thought (implicit, emotional). You say it is time for the Pledge of Allegiance, and your class immediately rises (implicit, procedural). You then recall that last night's homework must be turned in and ask your students to do so (explicit, semantic). They begin to pass their papers up the row (implicit, procedural).

As you can see from this scenario, you are constantly retrieving different types of memories. That's how your brain functions on a regular basis. It naturally draws upon what connections it can make for the current situation.

According to Pinker (1999), our brains will logically access memories that are useful, that have been repeated, and that require the least effort. Because memory works this way, it is imperative to take our students through the seven steps to provide the necessary repetition and ensure that memories become easy to access. Otherwise, the semantic memories that students require for assessment will be too difficult or impossible to access.

In this chapter, we will examine several factors affecting how well our students retrieve information. False memory, test anxiety, instruction/assessment mismatch, and location can each influence the ability to retrieve long-term memories.

What Is Retrieval?

Retrieval of memory in its most universal form is the ability to bring a past event or prior knowledge to one's mind. It is this conscious recollection that we call *memory*. Oftentimes this is called *declarative memory* because we can actually declare it (Squire & Kandel, 2008). Real-life acts of memory usually involve deciding what kind of information is useful at the moment and then selecting that information out of all that we know. We make these decisions all day long (Goldberg, 2001), as shown in the scenario at the start of the chapter.

When we test our students for facts, *we* are making the decision of what they are to recall. For instance, I may give a basic memory test to participants at a presentation. I may offer them a list of words, ask them to remember them, and then later ask them to write them down. When the decision of what is to be remembered is given to the *participant*, we add higher-level thinking processes. The frontal lobes are involved in the decision.

The 4th grade students had been studying the Civil War. Their teacher, Miss Dees, had been focusing on identifying similarities and differences. She had guided the students through several Venn diagrams investigating generals, battles, uniforms, forms of fighting, and reasons for fighting. The students wrote reflection papers to go with each visual representation.

Miss Dees used several formative assessments throughout the unit. Students presented their diagrams with brief oral remarks. Miss Dees gave a vocabulary quiz to ascertain whether the students understood all the important words in the unit.

For her summative assessment at the end of the unit, she wanted to assess their understanding. The students had performed well on the individual assessments, and now Miss Dees wanted to uncover their ability to take the memories and use them by applying them in a different way.

The assessment began as follows: "You have been using Venn diagrams to represent the differences and similarities between various aspects of the Civil War. One of the areas we studied was the boredom that soldiers suffered when they were not in battle. Compare and contrast what the soldiers in the Civil War did to handle their boredom with the ways you use to alleviate boredom."

Miss Dees was the decision maker on the vocabulary quiz. The students knew exactly what they were to study or memorize. For the oral presentation, the students could use higher levels of thinking to create and make their presentations. They chose the similarities and differences. In the last assessment, decision making again went to the students. Though the assessment did not specifically say to use a Venn diagram, many did so. Others created a Venn diagram as a prewriting component and then wrote a paragraph. For this higher-level assessment, the students had to access the procedural knowledge of identifying similarities and differences and their conceptual knowledge of what boredom is and how it is encountered and acted upon in two different aspects of life, in two eras in history, and, in some cases, by two different age groups.

 Mental Note: Retrieval is the ability to access long-term memories, bring then into the working memory process, and solve problems.

How Do We Retrieve?

Many people claim that they have trouble accessing memories. We know from previous steps that you cannot recall information that you never stored. Active participation encourages learning and memory storage, whereas inattention does not. Where there is no storage, there can be no retrieval. If no effort is being made to record new information for later, then our interests and preferences influence the strength and even the nature of the memory. When we wish to remember, intending to hold onto information for a later result, the probability of having a lasting memory is increased.

According to Squire and Kandel (2008), "Memory appears to be stored in the same distributed assembly of brain structures that are engaged in initially perceiving and processing what is to be remembered" (p. 72). These neuroscientists suggest that the availability of the memory may depend on the *strength* of the cue provided. Let's say you are asked to recall the plot of a novel you recently read by being offered the cue, "You know, the one about the woman whose husband dies and she marries that guy." The cues here are woman, dead husband, and second marriage. These may seem like enough triggers to jog anyone's memory, but many novels have similar plots. If the rememberer is to differentiate one novel from another, dissimilar characteristics are necessary. According to Sousa (2017), we tend to store information in networks by similarity but retrieve it back into working memory by difference. More specifically, the brain stores the attributes of information in a network with its characteristics. To retrieve the memory, the brain must somehow differentiate the information from all other stored information. It must find a difference that separates it from other networks. For example, the description of your best friend is stored in a network among descriptions of all of your friends. To access the correct information, the brain must find a difference. If you are walking down the street and see a familiar face in the distance, you may not initially know enough to name the individual. As the person gets closer, your brain realizes that it's not Marge, Carolyn, or Donna because the person's features are different than theirs. It must be Betty! Yes, that's who it is. Therefore, in the case of the novel, more specific cues may be necessary to remember which novel is being discussed; perhaps, "Do you remember the novel where the woman lost her husband in the Civil War? She was from the South, and later she marries a Northerner?" These added details offer some of the specific attributes of the novel.

False Memories

It was a simple test. I read a list of words to my students at an average pace. I asked them not to write down any of the words but rather to just sit back and listen. They would not be asked to write down as many as they could remember.

"Blanket, snore, sofa, lullaby, doze, awake, snooze, slumber, peace, yawn, drowsy, dream, tired." I looked up from my list and chatted with my students for about 20 seconds to let the echo of my words pass from their immediate memory.

"OK, raise your hand if you heard me say the word door," *I asked. No one raised a hand.*

"Good. I didn't say the word door. *Raise your hand if you heard me say the word* awake."

A few students raised their hands. I nodded. "Yes, I did say the word awake. *Raise your hand if you heard me say the word* sleep."

Almost every hand went up. I shook my head. "I didn't say the word sleep." *At this, the students were amazed.*

"What made you believe I said sleep?" *I asked.*

"You tricked us," Blair said. "You said a lot of words that we think of in relation to sleep."

Blair was correct. What she did not realize was that I intentionally gave my students a false memory. I activated the network of neurons that had been organized in their brains around the concept of sleep. Because I mentioned so many cues for sleep, they believed they had heard it.

This activity was one I had seen Daniel Schacter do many times during his presentations. Giving false memories to others may be difficult to avoid at all times. But it is something we must be aware of when it comes to memory retrieval and assessments. Forced-choice assessments consisting of multiple choice and true/false questions may easily lead students to false memories.

Here's another activity that shows how easily we are swayed by the activated networks in memory storage. Tell your students that you are going to give them 10 quick questions, and they are to answer orally as quickly as possible. Then quickly hold up a sheet of white paper and ask, "What color is this paper?" The students will all say white. Then quickly ask, "What do cows drink?" Most students will answer milk. Some might realize their mistake and discuss why they fell for it. Their brains were preprogrammed to think of something white. During a timed test, a network could be activated and cause similar mistakes.

Remind your students to read test questions carefully. If they are multiple-choice, each possible answer must be read in its entirety. These questions begin with a stem and then offer several choices, usually three or four. Only one is the best answer; the others are called *distracters*. And they are meant to do just that—distract the test-taker. They may consist of partially correct answers. If the correct part is at the beginning of the distracter, it may activate a network with inaccurate information that causes the student to mark it as the right answer.

Similar situations may occur with true/false questions. It is possible to start each statement with a truth or partial truth, but the ending makes the difference. These types of questions also should be read entirely to ensure accuracy.

> ☀ **Mental Note: Activating networks of neurons may elicit false connections in your students' minds.**

Test Anxiety

Test anxiety is a form of stress. Many of us have *eustress*, or good stress, when we take an exam. It gets some adrenaline pumping and actually assists in our recovery of memories. Some students, however, can become overwhelmed by test anxiety.

According to stress physiologist Robert Sapolsky (2012), stress is best handled when five factors are present:

1. **Predictability:** Do students know what kind of assessment they are facing? Are they familiar with the content? Have there been enough rehearsals and reviews?
2. **Choice:** Are there any options for the student? This may be as simple as offering three essay questions but only requiring that two be answered.

3. **A Feeling of Control:** This is present when a student understands the goal of the assessment and has rehearsed and reviewed properly.

4. **Social Interaction:** If the environment is such that the students feel that they are "in this together," they will feel less threatened by a test. Perhaps students can even take group assessments when appropriate.

5. **Physical Activity:** Of course, we don't want students jumping around during a test, but it might be wise to offer some movement activities before testing. Stiggins suggests that students be involved in assessments, describing several ways to do so (see Figure 7.1).

FIGURE 7.1	**Levels of Student Involvement with Assessment**

Low-Level Involvement				⟶			High-Level Involvement	
Takes assessment/ gets grade	Is allowed to offer comments on test improvement	Constructs assessment tasks	Assists with scoring criteria	Creates scoring standard	Self-evaluates using scoring measures	Understands assessment/ evaluation effects	Relates teacher assessment and self-assessment to academic achievement

Adapted from Stiggins (2001).

It can also help to discuss students' specific fears with them and offer ways they can be addressed. If a student is afraid of forgetting, for example, perhaps some mnemonics will provide some confidence. If the fear revolves around difficult questions, tell the student to answer the easiest first. Some students are stressed about time limits. Pacing is an important part of testing. Standardized tests are usually timed, and classroom assessments are often given under some time constraints. Chapman and King (2000) suggest providing students with some possible pacing instructions or giving them timed tests for review. They also suggest adding a blank page at the end of your classroom assessment where students can write down what they know about the content. Sometimes students tell me, "I studied, but I focused on the wrong things!" This blank page lets them write down what they did study, and you can add, but never subtract, points for this information (Chapman & King, 2012).

What does test anxiety do to the student brain? Let's look at Charlie, a 4th grader who does not test well. Charlie has trouble falling asleep the night before the state test. He says that he doesn't do well on tests. (Someone told him that, and he believes adults.) He wakes up in the morning, and his mother prepares eggs for breakfast. A high-protein meal is good for attentiveness. Charlie nibbles at his breakfast, as his stomach is a bit queasy due to the chemicals in his body that have been released to protect him from the stressor. In caveman days, stressors were wild animals, and the same chemicals were released in people back then. Our stressors are different, but our body and brain responses remain the same. Charlie knows this test somehow "counts," and he is dealing with cortisol being released. Cortisol in small amounts is good, but in large amounts it increases the stressful feelings. When enough cortisol is released, working memory prepares for the action that might take place as the stress response causes us to want to fight, flee, or freeze. When Charlie takes his test, he remembers his past frustration and poor performances, which makes his adrenal glands pump more cortisol into his body. Working memory is focused on the past and connects with long-term memory to access the bad memories of test taking. Charlie is unable to focus because working memory is busy, and he is unable to access prior knowledge, as long-term memory is sending down scenes from past testing experience. Most kids don't fight or flee under these circumstances, but they certainly freeze. This kind of experience calls for some major interventions.

☀ **Mental Note: Discuss with your students ways to deal with test anxiety.**

One common problem with retrieval occurs when the instructional strategies used do not match the reviews or the assessment. Different vocabulary, levels of complexity, or a transfer problem from one memory pathway to another can cause this difficulty.

Vocabulary

The vocabulary issue affects both standardized and classroom assessments. In the former, high-frequency words are used that may be unfamiliar to many of our students. Popham (2001) notes that children from affluent, educationally oriented families "grow up routinely hearing the words and phrases that form the items on standardized achievement tests. That's especially true if the tests deal with language arts, where you'll find item after item in which the child who grew up in a family where 'proper' English was used has a tremendous leg up over children whose parents' first language wasn't English or whose parents spoke English in a 'non-standard' manner" (p. 57).

For classroom assessment, we must keep in mind that our verbal vocabulary may or may not be in the memory lexicon of our students. Hearing us use words that they do not see in print until the assessment may confuse and disorient our students. They must also be able to pronounce the words themselves if we want them to use them in a recall exercise or recognize them on a recognition test (Schenck, 2011). For our young or struggling readers, this point is very important.

Susan was working hard teaching her 6th graders, while also pursuing her master's program. This semester, she was taking a course on curriculum alignment. For her next class, Susan was to bring in a classroom assessment for the group to review that matched the state standards and met certain criteria.

Susan was just finishing a novel unit on Wringer *by Jerry Spinelli. She was preparing the final assessment, a paper-and-pencil test. She had used an anticipation guide to begin the unit. The students had discussed the chapters in small groups, generated their own questions, role-played some of the scenes, and had large-group discussions. They understood the facts, such as that a "wringer" in this story is a 10-year-old boy who is expected to wring the necks of pigeons at the town's annual Pigeon Day. Susan was certain that the students understood the novel's underlying theme of coming of age. She included the following questions in her assessment:*

- *What does the recurring image of gunsmoke tell us about Palmer's anxiety?*
- *Why does Palmer feel compelled to ignore Dorothy or tease her in public when privately he holds much respect for her?*

- *Even though most 10-year-olds in his town consider it an honor to be a wringer, why does Palmer abhor this tradition?*

Susan was excited about her thought-provoking questions, but was greatly disappointed in the responses. Frustrated, she took her assessment and student samples to her graduate class. The group found her assessment to be well aligned with the standards.

"Then why did they do so poorly?" Susan asked her classmates. "I am very disappointed. You should have heard the discussion. They summarized some of the chapters and paraphrased the others. We found text-to-self connections. I really thought this would be a wonderful representation of what they had learned."

Susan's instructor led the entire group in a discovery process. First, they loosely defined the concept of mismatching instruction and assessment. Then the teachers looked carefully at the vocabulary in Susan's questions. When asked whether she had used the words *compelling*, *abhors*, and *recurring* in her lessons, Susan couldn't remember. She knew the concepts had been covered, but she wondered whether she had subconsciously used a more sophisticated vocabulary because she was bringing the assessment in to be reviewed by her peers. It is quite possible that we create an assessment using vocabulary that we use naturally and assume others use as well.

Mental Note: Use good academic vocabulary words in classroom discourse and on formative assessments so that when you use them on summative assessments, students will have no trouble with them.

Levels of Complexity

Sousa (2015) differentiates between levels of difficulty and levels of complexity. *Complexity* refers to the type of thought processes used to handle information and problems. *Difficulty* is the amount of effort needed within a level of complexity. Using the new Bloom's taxonomy (Anderson et al., 2001), *complexity* may be defined as the levels of thinking involved. The more complex a task is, the higher the level of thinking required. The more difficult a task is, the more effort is used at a particular level of thinking (see Figure 7.2).

FIGURE 7.2	Bloom's Taxonomy in Determining Levels of Complexity and Difficulty in Thought Process

Levels of Complexity →

	Remember	Understand	Apply	Analyze	Evaluate	Create
Level of Difficulty	↓	↓	↓	↓	↓	↓

When it comes to complexity, many testing companies turn to Webb's Depth of Knowledge (DOK) rather than Bloom. Whereas the DOK model focuses on cognitive demands and the thinking process, Bloom focuses on the tasks students complete based on the verb used in the taxonomy. Bloom uses verbs that are particular to each level of the taxonomy while Webb recycles the verbs depending on the expectation of each level of thinking. For instance, level 1 in the DOK model involves recall and automatic responses from students. One of the cognitive processes for recall is *explain.* This level is meant to answer the question, "What is the knowledge?" Level 2 involves conceptual thinking, which increases in complexity and requires students to go beyond recall. It is meant to answer the question, "How can the knowledge be used?" The verb *explain* is also used at this level. What would the tasks look like using *describe* at each level? At level 1, the question might be "Describe who was the major character." At level 2, the question might be "Describe the relationship between the main character and his enemy." Level 3 is meant to answer the question, "How can the knowledge be used?" and level 4 to answer the question, "How else can the knowledge be used?" For Webb, what follows the verb determines the level of complexity (Francis, 2016).

Rehearsals and reviews must match the assessment in complexity. In general, rehearsals begin at the lower levels of the taxonomy for learning or levels 1 and 2 in Webb's DOK, and then progress to more complex activities and exercises. By the final rehearsals and concluding review, be sure that the complexity level is equal to the assessment. The new generation of tests requires students to answer questions from Webb's DOK level 2 and above.

Using Susan's novel unit on *Wringer,* Figure 7.3 illustrates some possible questions with increasing complexity and added difficulty.

FIGURE 7.3	Using the Novel *Wringer* to Illustrate Bloom's Revised Taxonomy					
	Remember	Understand	Apply	Analyze	Evaluate	Create
Complexity	Who are the main characters in *Wringer?*	Why is Palmer upset about turning 10?	Compare the pigeon information in *Wringer* to that on one of the websites listed.	What are the components of the tradition that Palmer has difficulty with?	Is Pigeon Day and the shooting of 5,000 birds a justified event to pay for the park's maintenance?	Design an alternative process that represents coming of age and will also fulfill the other results on Pigeon Day.
Difficulty	Describe their personalities.	Describe the reactions of two others in the book about turning 10.	Compare the pigeon information to three other sources, including one website.	Take those components and prioritize them from the most offensive to the least offensive.	Include the amount of money gained and how it is specifically used.	Create an agenda for the process that can be used by the townspeople.

 Mental Note: Students who encounter a complexity level beyond what has been rehearsed and reviewed may underperform on an assessment.

Transfer

The unit had gone really well. The students were attentive from the beginning, when Mr. Perez introduced the Bill of Rights by showing a clip from the movie Born Yesterday, *in which Melanie Griffith's character learns the amendments by writing a song to the tune of "The 12 Days of Christmas." The students loved it! Mr. Perez and the students wrote their own song to the same tune and included only the Bill of Rights.*

Mr. Perez also put the students in groups and had each group create a visual for an amendment. They had to present their visual and explain it. To be certain they knew the amendments, students created an "amendment dance." They had different movements for each amendment. For review, they played "Amendment Pursuit," modeled after Trivial Pursuit. Mr. Perez divided the class into two teams. He read the questions. As long as the team answered correctly, they could continue answering questions until they "Filled the Bill" by reaching 10 points. They also played a Password game using vocabulary from the amendments. This was to ensure their understanding of the wording of each amendment. The culminating activity was role-playing each amendment. The students also did this in groups.

The assessment Mr. Perez designed was a paper-and-pencil test. It contained multiple-choice, matching, true/false, and short-answer questions. Many students did not do well.

The assessment for this unit was not a good match for the instruction. Even though Mr. Perez had designed the assessment before he designed his instructional strategies, he did little to help the students store and practice information in the semantic pathway. They learned through the emotional pathway (role-playing), through the procedural pathway (dance), and through the conditioned-response pathway (song, games). But at no time did he ask them to take the information that they had stored and recode it in writing. His choices were to give more writing exercises to help the students get the information into the right pathway or to use some of the activities as authentic assessments using appropriate scoring rubrics. To do the former, after each activity, the students could write a summary of what they did or do some peer teaching.

Because the brain tries to make sense of any information it is given, it takes the offered cues and begins searching. In this Bill of Rights unit, the students were searching a dead end. Perhaps if the assessment had referred them to the dance, song, and games, the students would have been able to access the information more easily. I am not saying that Mr. Perez should not have taught the unit this way; it was very effective to get the students involved. With just a few more steps in the plan, however, the assessment results would likely have been more impressive.

> ☀ **Mental Note: Retrieval will be faster if assessment matches the memory pathways used for instruction and assessment.**

Location! Location! Location!

I was in the gym with the cheerleaders. This was one of the few after-school practices we had in the large gymnasium where our games were played. The basketball coach would only give up this gym once every couple of weeks. Today, the basketball teams were practicing in the small gym.

The girls had to rearrange themselves. They were much closer together for our other practices, and I was helping them center themselves. They had a new dance routine to practice for this Saturday's game, as well as their cheers.

"Mrs. Sprenger, we've never done this dance in here," Christine announced frantically. "I always focused on the picture of the school while I was dancing. There's not a picture in here!"

"Don't worry, Christine, we'll be practicing every morning in here this week. Find another focal point and you'll be fine," I replied.

The squad was set. I turned to start the music when I saw Keisha coming through the door. I had forgotten that I would give her a makeup quiz tonight after school.

She looked at me disapprovingly. "You aren't in your room. I've been waiting for you. If Mr. Bell hadn't seen me and told me where you were, I'd still be sitting there. This is the only night I can stay late and make up the quiz."

I apologized for my forgetfulness. I opened my grade book and pulled out a copy of the quiz. Now, where can she take it? I wondered to myself. I don't want her back in the classroom without me. I'm afraid she'll look up the answers. It'll be too noisy in here. I checked the coach's office, which was empty.

"Keisha, go into Mr. Blundy's office and close the door," I said. "You can take your quiz in there. If the music is too loud, let me know."

Keisha obeyed, and I went back to coaching the cheerleaders. Several minutes passed, and Keisha returned.

"Finished already?" I asked. "Or is the noise bothering you?"

"It's not the noise, Mrs. Sprenger. It's the office. I can't think in there. I can't remember anything. I need to be in your room. I need my desk, and I need to see your chalkboard."

"There's nothing on the chalkboard, Keisha," I replied. "There are no answers there."

"They come into my head when I look at it. That's how I take all my tests," she insisted.

I left the cheerleaders and took Keisha to my room. It wasn't fun or easy, but I ran back and forth between my two responsibilities. Mr. Blundy came into the gym and offered to keep an eye on the cheerleaders. Keisha finished her quiz quickly. She did very well.

I was fascinated with Keisha's comments. I started observing students taking tests in my room. My "action" research was compelling. I copied my class lists and started keeping some records of what students did when they were taking tests or quizzes, writing essays, and doing worksheets. I found that about 30 percent of the 8th graders became totally absorbed in what they were doing. I never saw them look around. About 40 percent glanced up occasionally but didn't seem to be looking at anything in particular. Another 15 to 20 percent looked at the chalkboard or at me every so often. But 5 to 10 percent of my students had to look at the chalkboard, the overhead screen, the bulletin board, or me every few minutes! Keisha was one of them.

The research on this phenomenon is persuasive. As far back as 1690, John Locke described a case of a young man who learned to dance in a room with an old trunk. He found that he could not remember dance steps without the presence of that trunk (Baddeley, 1999). As far as testing is concerned, it appears that recognition tests, which provide a certain number of cues, do not rely on the environment as much as recall tests do.

Two years ago, I had the opportunity to see this phenomenon played out in a state testing situation. A principal in a nearby community called me, very concerned about his school's writing test results. He wanted me to work with the teachers. I asked to see copies of the students' essays from the state assessment, and he was able to acquire some. All it took was for me to see that the students wrote insufficiently. The state did not have enough writing on each essay for them to know whether they could meet the standards.

"Where did these students take this test?" I asked the principal and the teachers. As someone pulled out the testing schedule, the 8th grade teacher started nodding his head. "They took the test in their homerooms. So some of them were with social studies teachers, some with science teachers, and some with math teachers," he announced. "Only my homeroom class was with me. I teach writing to 5th through 8th grades."

Examining the test scores of those students who happened to be in the language arts classroom, I could easily reach some interesting conclusions. Many more of the students who were writing in their writing classroom met or exceeded the standards. They simply wrote more. The environment and the presence of their writing teacher helped them connect to the writing expectations for an adequate essay. The other content area teachers did not expect extensive essays in their subjects, so the students wrote shorter pieces.

This experience led us to a discussion about expectations and common vocabulary. Why this experience occurred this particular year with these students, no one could say for certain. Perhaps the schedules had been different in the past. Perhaps these students were more sensitive to their environment.

As I travel and share this information with administrators and teachers, I ask them to consider the possibilities. We would assume that with the proper amount of rehearsal and review, transfer would not be an issue. In most cases, it is not. But for some students, transfer may take more time. The consolidation of semantic memory is different for all of us. As Eichenbaum and Dickerson (2010) suggest, we take the episodes and extract the meaning that becomes a solid semantic memory. Because of differing brain development, attention, motivation, and experiences, I believe it behooves us to offer students every opportunity to perform well in a situation with such high stakes for us all.

> ☀ **Mental Note: Students who learn information in one location may retrieve it more readily in the same location.**

Assessment Methods and Retrieval

It is important to review the two major types of assessment. *Formative* assessment is generally used within the classroom as a form of feedback to improve and increase learning. This may include paper-and-pencil tests, personal communication, performances, and portfolios. *Summative* assessment is a measure of what students have learned at a certain period in time and may include a unit or chapter test and state or national achievement tests. All of these assessments should be aligned with the state or national standards. For the purpose of transfer, these assessments should focus on more than factual information. These should involve complex thinking at levels 3 or 4 of the DOK model.

Performance Assessment

When students demonstrate what they know through a performance, retrieval is dependent on the type of performance assessment. Danielson (2002) describes two types: spontaneous and structured. A *spontaneous* performance may be through informal observation of the student during the rehearsal stage of learning. Anecdotal records may be kept, and rubrics may be used as well. O'Connor (2009) contends that only a student's most recent effort should receive a grade, not the trials to reach that level. He also believes that we should be discussing the grading methodology with the students when we begin a new unit of study.

Structured authentic assessment is set up with the student prior to the performance. Students should have a rubric to guide them so they know exactly how they will be evaluated. In this way, students are well prepared, and retrieval is not normally an issue. Keep in mind, however, that performance anxiety, like test anxiety, can be a strong factor in how well the information necessary to perform is retrieved. If students are performing in front of the class, public speaking may be an issue. Because offering students choices may lower stress levels, allowing them to pick the mode of performance assessment may help. Those terribly uncomfortable with an oral presentation may choose an essay, videotape, or some other product as a way to demonstrate their knowledge.

Traditional Tests

Paper-and-pencil tests usually require students to work independently. They also have time limits and usually restrict the use of any outside resources, such as notes. The retrieval cues included on the assessment must be enough to trigger facts, concepts, and procedures. Therefore, it is imperative to use the right format to ascertain the information that is required. For instance, a constructed-response test, such as an essay test, may be a better way to evaluate a student's ability to use the higher-level thinking skills of analyzing, applying, and evaluating. Different formats may be more suitable for factual knowledge, procedural knowledge, and conceptual knowledge (Danielson, 2002; Stiggins, 2004).

Selected-response tests include multiple-choice, matching, and true/false questions. These are best for measuring a student's ability to retrieve facts and isolated concepts, although it is possible to construct selected-response tests to determine whether students can analyze, apply, and evaluate what they learn.

Constructed-response tests require students to construct their own answers rather than choose the correct ones. These consist of fill-in-the-blank assessments and essays. This type of test can measure larger conceptual understandings, problem solving, and higher-level processes.

☀ **Mental Note: Choosing the appropriate assessment may make the difference between successful and unsuccessful retrieval.**

When Retrieval Fails

If you have followed the seven steps in this book, what do you do if there are students who still can't retrieve the information and understandings you expect? Ask yourself the following questions:

1. **Did you step back?** Did you begin with the end in mind? If you created your assessment based on the expectations, enduring understandings, and essential questions, then your students will have fewer retrieval problems. We sometimes have a tendency to change directions as we proceed through a unit.

2. **Are your students reflecting throughout the unit?** Are you battling time and, as a result, skimping on reflection time? Check your reflection habits. Curriculum is often accused of being a mile wide and an inch deep. *Give your students the opportunity to make deep connections through reflections.*

3. **Are you providing enough reinforcement?** Research shows that the most powerful effect on student achievement is instructional reinforcement (Cotton, 2000). Check to see whether you are providing the feedback your students need to correct misconceptions and strengthen memory connections. Make use of peer evaluations and computer-based instructional reinforcement that provide immediate feedback.

4. **Are you varying your rehearsal strategies to meet diverse needs?** The need for differentiation is great. Check your rehearsal strategies for various modes of learning. If you find you must reteach, try rehearsals that meet needs you may not have met the first time around. Make the most of students' strengths and guide them through their weaknesses.

5. **Are you spacing your reviews appropriately?** Consult the chart in Chapter 6 on spacing reviews. Make sure you are including reviews throughout the unit. If you are suspicious of student understanding, insert another review before moving on.

6. **Have you reflected on your teaching experience?** I don't know if I ever felt that I had executed the ideal unit. There was always something I learned as I taught, and I made changes every time. The only way to improve is to reflect and make adjustments. Forgive yourself if

you have to reteach and reassess. Researchers have found that reteaching is critical for the students who require it to master learning material (Cotton, 2000).

The Effects of Retrieval on Memory

It is the recovery of long-term memories in working memory that allows us to make new connections. Conceptual understandings and procedural understandings can then be reapplied in new and unusual circumstances. According to Squire and Kandel (2008), when material is well learned initially, forgetting occurs gradually. Memory works by extracting the meaning of what we encounter. Out of many rehearsals and reviews, memory is established but later can be modified by new information and by the rehearsal process itself. Memory also can be distorted by how it is examined in a retrieval test.

Each time we retrieve memories, we reconstruct them and review them. If rehearsal strategies have allowed us to rework memories using higher-level thinking processes, we can build on those experiences and apply the information again in similar situations.

Reflection

1. The ability to retrieve information quickly and easily offers students a feeling of self-confidence. How do you reinforce these feelings in every student in your classroom?
2. Some students are naturally slow processors and retrievers. What do you do in your classroom to provide them with the optimal environment for assessment and retrieval?
3. A constant reminder: Does what you are accepting as evidence that your students have enduring understanding match your instructional strategies?
4. Consider the state exam that is given at your school. At which level of Webb's DOK are the questions?

8

Realization

Carolyn was teaching writing again. She had 7th graders, so this was not a testing year for writing. She created a Writer's Workshop for her students, which would allow them to clearly see their writing change. Through different levels of group work and conferencing, she took the opportunity to help her students grow as writers. She created her own rubrics through the years, and assessing student writing was second nature to her.

The new principal entered Carolyn's room one day and handed her a flyer from the State Board of Education. It described a workshop on writing and using the state rubric. He asked that she attend with several other language arts teachers.

The day of the workshop, she was bowled over. Her rubric and the state's did not match. She didn't know how many areas she was missing that the state thought important enough to be assessing. Because she was teaching in between testing years, no one had put a lot of pressure on her. She knew her students progressed well in writing according to her standards. As the day wore on, it became clear that there were many things she didn't know.

Carolyn returned to her classroom the following day. In her hands she held the state rubric and many handouts explaining each characteristic. Although she had the information, applying it seemed like a monumental task. As she distributed the rubrics to the students and started explaining, she began to see the similarities to

her own rubric. She also began to make connections to what was happening at the
Writing Matters website and in the state standards.

It was hard to make changes, but finally everything fell into place. Carolyn's
expectations for writing had changed. Through a lot of experiences, her new learn-
ing became her new habits for teaching writing.

We have all had the experience of going from the awkward realization that we don't know anything to a feeling of competence. I was in high school the first time I heard the following saying: "Freshmen don't know and don't know they don't know. Sophomores don't know and know they don't know. Juniors know and don't know they know. Seniors know and know they know."

And so it is with educators and other professionals. Before we are exposed to learning models and strategies that are scientifically based, we don't know. When the exposure begins, we realize how much we don't know. As we begin the process of learning through professional development, but before we actually try things out in the classroom, we don't know that we know. Then, through actual classroom practice, we know. We develop a level of proficiency.

Summing Up the Seven Steps

Repetition is good for the brain. At least, that's what I tell my children when they tell me that I'm repeating myself! A short summary of each step in this book follows.

Step 1: Reach and Teach

Your attention and motivational skills may not need an "extreme make-over." Many of your current unit plans may just need some tweaking. We need to remember that novelty is appealing to our students, especially ado-lescents, who are primed to crave new sensations and new experiences (Arm-strong, 2016). All brains are programmed to respond to novelty, and that is one way to reach and teach our students. In Chapter 1, you learned that the following help reach students and provide the first step toward long-term retention and transfer, getting information into sensory memory:

- Attention
- Motivation
- Emotion
- Meaning
- Relationships
- Novelty
- Advance organizers
- Relevancy

☀ **Mental Note: If you can't reach 'em, you can't teach 'em!**

Step 2: Reflect

Offering students the opportunity to make connections requires that we give them some time to do so. This step reminds us that educators need to be aware of wait time, focus time, and reflection time. Reflection allows students to search their memories for prior knowledge that they may have about the topic. By manipulating the new information in working memory, they connect it with older, long-term memories. This allows them to find a "hook" to hang new information on. Here, again, are the seven habits of successful reflection:

1. Question
2. Visualization
3. Journaling
4. Thinking directives
5. PMI charts
6. Collaboration
7. Four-corner reflection

☀ **Mental Note: Reflection is not a luxury; it's a necessity.**

Step 3: Recode

While information is still in working memory, students must have the opportunity to put it in their own words. Research suggests that we remember better what we have produced. If our students can generate their own explanation of the concept, then it will be time to put the information into long-term storage. If the information is not clear to the student, the teacher can clear up any misconceptions or reteach. This is an opportunity to employ scientifically based research to help our students achieve. The following strategies are recommended for recoding:

- Interpreting
- Exemplifying
- Classifying
- Summarizing
- Inferring
- Comparing
- Explaining
- Using nonlinguistic representations

> ☀ **Mental Note: Self-generated material is better remembered.**

Step 4: Reinforce

At this step in the process, we let students know whether they understand the facts, concepts, or procedures. By assessing their recoding attempt without grading it and giving appropriate feedback, we can clear up misconceptions. The three types of feedback used to reinforce are motivational feedback, informational feedback, and developmental feedback.

> ☀ **Mental Note: Feedback is vital to learning.**

Step 5: Rehearse

Once students can put concepts, facts, and procedures into their own words accurately, it is time to begin to transfer it to long-term memory. There are five memory pathways, various learning styles, and multiple intelligences approaches to use. Rote rehearsal is useful for some facts, but elaborative rehearsal provides more meaning. Multiple rehearsals are necessary. Accurate recoding only sets up a network of neurons in students' brains. It has not been practiced, so it will not become a permanent memory without some repetition and manipulation. This step takes the information from working memory and places it throughout the brain, so it can be more easily accessed. Concepts to keep in mind from this step include the following:

- Rote rehearsal
- Elaborative rehearsal
- Sleep
- Spacing
- Homework and practice
- Multiple pathways
- Multiple episodes

Mental Note: We remember better the more fully we process new subject matter.

Step 6: Review

Whereas rehearsal puts information in long-term memory, review presents the opportunity to retrieve that information and manipulate it in working memory. The products of the manipulation can then be returned to long-term memory. Timing of review is important. It is necessary to space reviews closely at first, then farther apart. Here are some recommendations for this step:

- Match the review to instruction and assessment.
- Check for accuracy of the memory.

- Give students the conditions to use higher-level thinking skills to analyze, evaluate, and possibly create alternative ways to use the knowledge.
- Strengthen existing networks.
- For high-stakes testing, practice similar questions under similar conditions.
- Avoid cramming.

 Mental Note: Without review, most information will be lost from memory.

Step 7: Retrieve

The ability to access long-term memories, bring them into the working memory process, and solve problems is the culmination of the memory-building process. Retrieval is most successful when the context and the cues that were present when the material was first learned are the same as the context and the cues that are present later when making an attempt to recall. The following concepts are covered in this step:

- Type of assessment
- Specific cues
- Recognition techniques
- Recall strategies
- Stress

Mental Note: Memory retrieval may be dependent on cues.

Metacognition

Throughout this step-by-step process, students begin to discover how they learn and remember. By doing so, they naturally begin to reflect while learning. Some would assume that this alone is metacognition, or thinking about thinking. We often reflect after we have completed a task or assignment. This is a good thing to do, but metacognition is more than reflection. As Sousa (2017) says, "Metacognition refers to higher-order thinking where an individual has conscious control over the cognitive processes *while* learning" (p. 30). Marzano (2017) states that metacognition involves the exertion of executive control over the complex tasks that we endeavor to perform and lists the following teachable metacognitive skills: planning for goals and making adjustments, staying focused when answers and solutions are not immediately apparent, pushing the limits of one's knowledge and skills, generating and pursuing one's own standards of excellence, seeking incremental steps, seeking accuracy, seeking clarity, resisting impulsivity, and seeking cohesion and coherence. Marzano provides a scope and sequence for these skills as well.

The seven steps outlined in this book can help you teach metacognitive skills to your students. I have stressed the importance of reflection after each step, each rehearsal, and each review. The practice of reflecting about what we know, what we don't know, and how best to learn what we don't know will lead us to processing information at the appropriate level or step. As students reflect after each step, they will begin to think about what they are doing *during* each step. Metacognition will kick in as students think about how they want to work on their learning and advance up those steps to long-term memory. Our goal is to help solidify memories for long-term storage and transfer. See Figure 8.1 for a review of the seven steps.

During the first week of school, I teach my students about how the brain learns and remembers. I offer them the steps to building long-term memory and share mnemonic devices. I test their memories with simple assessments to make them feel successful. As we start each unit, I make sure the targets are clear and explain the process that we will go through to get the new facts, concepts, and procedures into long-term memory.

I like to ask my students, "How are you thinking?" I want them to be aware of their thinking processes and be able to articulate them. Once they can explain how they are thinking, they will begin to question themselves, paving the way for metacognition and development of metacognitive control.

FIGURE 8.1	The Seven Steps to Remembering

Step	Characteristics	Memory Process
1. Reach	Attention Motivation Emotion Learning styles	Sensory > Immediate
2. Reflect	Question Collaborate Visualize	Immediate > Working
3. Recode	Self-generate Symbolize Dialogue	Working
4. Reinforce	Feedback Reteach Reinvent	Working Emotional
5. Rehearse	Repeat Rote Elaborative Spacing	Working > Long-term
6. Review	Matching instruction Anticipated problems Unanticipated problems	Long-term > Working > Long-term
7. Retrieve	Assessment Cues Stress/test anxiety	Long-term > Working Emotional memory

Figure 8.2 shows an if-then chart to help assess where a student is in the memory-building process and which step to go to next. Students can also use this chart to self-assess. Once they truly know their own memory processes and strengths, they will be able to figure out what they need to do next.

FIGURE 8.2	An If-Then Chart to Assess Students' Needs					
If a student cannot recognize the material . . .	If a student cannot put the facts, concept, or procedure in his own words but can repeat yours . . .	If a student can't recall during a review . . .	If a student cannot recall on a practice quiz . . .	If a student can recognize but not recall . . .	If a student can recode but has difficulty with rehearsals . . .	If a student can apply, analyze, and evaluate . . .
Go back to step 1, reach.	Go back to step 2, reflect.	Go back to step 3, recode.	Give a recognition quiz.	Go back to step 3, recode, and try a new recoding process.	Go back to step 4, reinforce, and offer developmental feedback.	Go to step 5, rehearse, and add creativity or another level of complexity; or review, assess, and move on.

☀ **Mental Note: Metacognition and metacognitive control occur when we ask ourselves "How am I thinking?"**

Exposure to Current Research

All educators need to be aware of the scientifically-based research on teaching strategies, as well as the latest cognitive science research on how the brain learns and remembers. As Willis (2012) notes, "Students thrive in classrooms where teachers have the added tools from their neuroscience understanding. The result is nothing less than reigniting the joys of learning, even when they have been extinguished for years." According to Schenck (2011), 75 percent of a student's performance is based on what occurs prior to review and assessment. Motivation, attention, recoding, reinforcement, and rehearsals make up three-quarters of a student's grade. The other 25 percent is a combination of the reviews and the assessment itself.

Educators must have access to current studies and publications that will enhance their ability to encourage students' memories and understandings.

As a classroom teacher, you become an expert. With the proper background knowledge, you will be able to select the appropriate tools to engage your students and enhance their understanding. Experimental studies will provide overviews and advice based on current trends. Case studies will offer new instructional and assessment methods to consider. A multiple-year, cross-sectional study helps separate performance that is unique to a specific cohort (i.e., a group of students in a single grade) from performance that is related to teaching and other factors. Other studies, such as correlational ones, provide information about how variables affect each other.

Professional development for teachers indicates that a school district is interested not only in raising student achievement but also in providing teachers with the tools they need. It is not a sign that teachers need "fixing." Rather, it is an indication that the learning community is always open to learning more and better ways to assist in student understanding. One-shot professional development may offer a few strategies to use on Monday, but ongoing training with feedback will have a greater effect on changing old habits and developing more effective strategies that will be used in an automatic fashion. As teachers know, when the going gets tough, it is easy to fall back into old habits, even if they are ineffective. Just as our students need rehearsal and feedback to gain long-term understanding, so do we.

> **Mental Note: Teachers should be exposed to current scientific research about how the brain learns, remembers, and transfers.**

Retention or Retention?

If students are unable to retain the necessary information to demonstrate their ability to meet or exceed state or national standards, should they be retained? In this age of accountability, is it simply a matter of knowledge retention or grade retention? The effectiveness of retaining students is questionable. According to an ASCD ResearchBrief (2004) on "Attention and Student Achievement," "Many school systems have begun taking a harder line with regard to promotion policy, retaining students who do not make sufficient academic progress—particularly in reading and math." Yet, reading researcher Sally Shaywitz (2003) says that retention is not effective. According to her research, students who are not retained are better off academically and emotionally.

Reading specialist Debra Johnson (2001) completed a review of current literature on the topic of social promotion and retention. She found that retention affects behavior, attitude, and attendance. Current literature and current practice suggests that the following five strategies may serve as alternatives to retention or social promotion:

- **Intensify learning.** Develop rigorous standards, clear targets, and a rich curriculum; provide knowledgeable and skilled teachers; and create meaningful learning experiences.
- **Ensure skilled teachers by providing professional development.** Ongoing, meaningful professional development can greatly affect student achievement.
- **Expand learning options.** Use ongoing assessment, differentiation, and brain-based teaching.
- **Assess to inform.** Use both formative and summative assessment as feedback for students and teachers.
- **Intervene early.** Offer increased instructional time, and provide alternate methods of learning.

The purpose of this book is retention—retaining meaningful information that will raise student achievement and prevent students from being held back a grade. The emotional effect of repeating grades can be traumatic. According to Sevener (1990), children view the thought of flunking a grade to be almost as stressful as the death of a parent or blindness. Shared expectations by students and teachers, reflection, rehearsal, reinforcement, and review can provide pertinent information to all stakeholders. Student promotion should be based on classroom assessment as well as high-stakes testing. Memory retention and transfer are our goals.

Success Breeds Success for Students and Teachers

As our students retain more knowledge, they put forth the effort to continue learning. I suggest that you ask your students to describe how they have learned something that they enjoy and in which they excel. Show them how their learning follows a pattern. As students climb the steps toward long-term memory, events build upon one another. Show success with each step by using a reinforcement plan that includes informational feedback in a visual representation. Let your students see and feel their successes.

You will also feel successful as your students achieve. A success cycle will form as they become more eager to learn and you become more comfortable with the learning and memory process. It will become easier for students to pinpoint problem areas and overcome them.

I encourage you to take the first step.

Reflection

1. As your own learning curve goes up through the seven steps, think about your own thinking. What steps in the process are easiest for you? Where can you find help for a difficult step?
2. How familiar are you with current research? Perhaps you can begin a book study group at your school.
3. Do you have a voice in your own professional development? Consider your needs and compare them with those of your colleagues.
4. Is teacher turnover a problem in your school? What kind of teacher mentoring is available in your district?
5. Could you be part of a teacher peer group or learning team to support each other in aligning instruction to the standards and teaching for memory to ensure success for more students?

Appendix A
Brain Briefing

This appendix reviews some basic structures and functions of the brain to help you understanding the memory process.

Lobes of the Brain

There are four major lobes of the brain (see Figure A.1). The brain is divided into a left and a right hemisphere, and each hemisphere contains its own side of the lobes. The left hemisphere is associated with details, whereas the right tends to get the "big picture." Because memories are stored in different areas of the brain, an understanding of the functions and locations of each is desirable.

Parietal: The parietal lobes are located toward the back of the top of your head. Here we find the ability to process sensory stimuli, spatial awareness, and some problem solving.

Occipital: The occipital lobes are located in the middle of the back of the brain. They process visual stimuli. Memories of objects, people, and so forth are kept here to provide meaning to new information and make sense of the visual world.

Temporal: The temporal lobes are located on the sides of your head, above your ears. They are responsible for auditory information, some memory, and some speech.

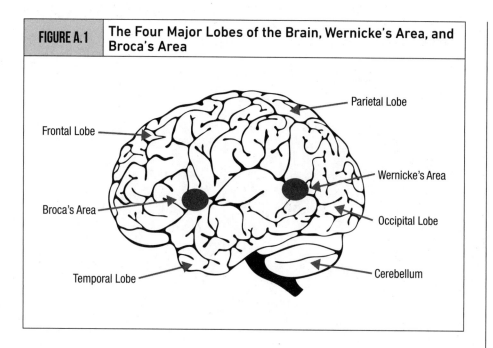

FIGURE A.1 | The Four Major Lobes of the Brain, Wernicke's Area, and Broca's Area

Frontal: The frontal lobes are located toward the front of the top of your head and behind your forehead. This large area of the brain is responsible for executive functions such as working memory, higher-level thinking, future planning, decision making, and making choices.

> ☀ **Mental Note: Memories are dispersed throughout the lobes of the brain.**

Structures

Within the brain are many structures with various functions relating to memory (see Figures A.1 and A.2). Even though their purposes appear to be specific to them, the brain is really a system of systems. Many brain areas work together to accomplish tasks and help us learn and remember.

FIGURE A.2 | Basic Structures in the Brain

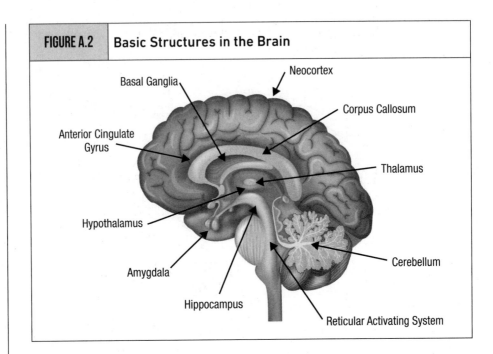

Amygdala: The amygdala is the almond-shaped structure in the middle of the brain. It is part of the area referred to as the *limbic system*. The amygdala processes emotion. It filters incoming information for emotional content and catalogs that information for future use.

Anterior cingulate: This structure, located in the frontal lobe, is associated with attention, emotion, motivation, and memory.

Basal ganglia: Part of the reward system in the brain, these structures deep within the cortex are also responsible for some of our memories. Evidence points to the basal ganglia as the primary site for learning sequential information (Bednark, Campbell, & Cunnington, 2015).

Broca's area: Located just behind the left temple, this area is associated with speech production, including vocabulary, syntax, and grammar (expressive language).

Cerebellum: The "little brain" is located beneath the occipital lobes in the back of the brain. Long thought to be associated only with balance, new research shows that this structure plays an important role in navigating movement and thought processes (Sousa, 2017).

Corpus callosum: A band of nerve fibers that connects the left and right sides of the brain, allowing for communication between both hemispheres.

Hippocampus: Close to the amygdala lies the hippocampus. Also a limbic structure, located deep in the temporal lobe, the hippocampus processes incoming information that is factual. This is a critical structure involved in facilitating the short-term to long-term memory process.

Neocortex: The top layer of the brain, the neocortex is one-fourth to one-eighth of an inch thick. It is here that many of our memories are stored in the different lobes.

Reticular activating system: This structure, located at the base of the brain, controls arousal. It connects the frontal lobes, limbic system, brain stem, and sense organs. The hippocampus also communicates with the reticular activating system. If this system overarouses us, the hippocampus can compare the information with the past and supervise events as either novel or commonplace (Sousa, 2017).

Thalamus: The thalamus is located in the middle of the brain and is sometimes considered part of the limbic system. This vital structure filters all incoming sensory information and relays it to the proper association area of each lobe.

Wernicke's area: Located in the left hemisphere, this region is thought to be responsible for language comprehension (receptive language).

☀ **Mental Note: Many structures are involved in the storage and retrieval of memories.**

The Information Highway

All sensory information enters our brain through the brain stem, except for the sense of smell, which is directly processed into the limbic system. This is why smells bring back powerful memories—they connect immediately to the amygdala and hippocampus.

The first filtering structure in the brain is the reticular activating system. It sifts through the information to determine what stimuli to focus on. How does it know what to focus on? There are some basics that it follows: Survival is first and foremost (ever try to concentrate when you're hungry?), novelty is next, and then comes the power of choice. We can attend to anything that we want to attend to. As I sit here typing on my keyboard, until I concentrate on how the keys feel against my fingers, that bit of information is overlooked. If there were syrup on one of the keys, my brain would instantly focus on this novel (and sticky!) experience. Our awareness of the purpose of this system will become more important when we discuss attention.

From the reticular activating system, information flows to the thalamus. Like the old switchboard operators, the thalamus connects the information with its primary destination: Visual information is directed to the occipital lobe, auditory information to the temporal lobe, and so forth. Each of these lobes has its own *association cortex* where the information is identified and associated with previous knowledge. Once this process is complete, the information returns to the middle of the brain, where the hippocampus and the amygdala can filter it. If the information is factual, the hippocampus will hold it until it can be stored in long-term memory in the neocortex; it also catalogs it to make it possible to access. If it is emotional content, the amygdala will do the same. After information is catalogued, it is redistributed to the sensory areas for long-term storage.

Cells

The approximately three pounds of brain tissue that we each possess contains several different kinds of brain cells. About 10 percent of the mass consists of cells called *neurons* (see Figure A.3). These cells learn and store memories. They connect to each other via an electrochemical bond and form networks. These networks are activated and store our memories.

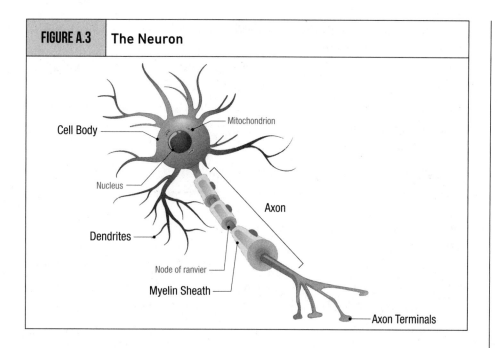

FIGURE A.3   **The Neuron**

Cell Body

Mitochondrion

Nucleus

Axon

Dendrites

Node of ranvier

Myelin Sheath

Axon Terminals

A neuron has formations called *dendrites*. These could be compared to branches on a tree. The dendrites receive information from other neurons. That information or message attaches itself to a receptor site on the dendrite. The message goes to the cell body and down the structure called the *axon*, which could be compared to the trunk of a tree. Each neuron has only one axon, but it can have thousands of dendrites. The axon will grow terminals (roots) in order to send multiple messages. When the message leaves the axon, it is in the form of a chemical, a *neurotransmitter*. This chemical crosses a space called a *synapse* and attaches itself to the dendrite of the next neuron.

When neurons communicate, they are said to "fire" (see Figure A.4). Although electrical activity is always occurring in the brain—that is, neurons are usually emitting low levels of electrical activity—when neurons are not firing rhythmically and purposefully, they are said to be "at rest." Neurons that fire together in a pattern are called *neural networks*. These networks form the patterns and programs in our brains. So, a memory requires a network of neurons to fire. You have stored millions of these networks.

The other 90 percent of the brain cells are called *glial cells*. *Glial* means "glue," and it describes many of the functions of these cells. They perform duties that nurture the neurons. Providing physical and nutritional support, glial cells hold neurons in place, transport nutrients, and digest debris. Their assistance provides strong connections between neurons, and without them memory would be affected (Sousa, 2017).

FIGURE A.4	Two Neurons Communicating

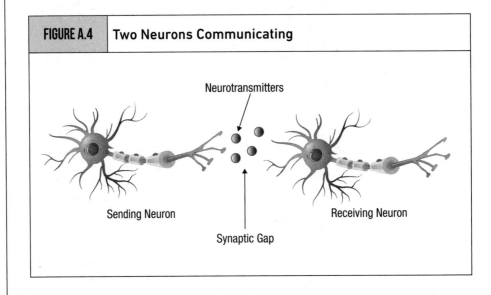

One particular type of glial cell insulates the neurons to speed the transmission of messages within the networks. This insulation is called *myelin*. It is a white lipid that is distributed throughout the brain in a developmental fashion (Armstrong, 2016). For instance, at birth, myelin has already developed in some brain areas such as those pertaining to hearing, some movement, and the sucking reflex. The last area of the brain to become "myelinated" is the prefrontal cortex, which is the frontal lobe area right behind the forehead. Once this is myelinated, decision making, future planning, and other higher-level functions become easier. This area, however, may not be completely coated with myelin until the mid-twenties!

Chemicals

The process of neurons communicating and setting up networks is electro-chemical. Within the neuron, the process is electrical, but between neurons, chemicals run the show. There are dozens of these chemicals, called *neurotransmitters*, in the brain. For memory purposes, we will isolate a few of them.

Acetylcholine. This chemical is vital to getting information into long-term memory. The levels are significantly higher when we sleep, supporting the theory that memories are reinforced during some of the sleep stages.

Dopamine. Dopamine is a neurotransmitter with several purposes in the brain. Many receptors for dopamine are found in the basal ganglia, part of the reward system. It is this system that profoundly affects long-term decision making and memories that run our lives. It affects movement, learning, pleasure, and reinforcement (Sousa, 2017).

Endorphin. This neurotransmitter is usually associated with the "runner's high," a feeling of euphoria from putting forth physical energy. It is also a necessary contributor to learning and memory.

GABA (gamma-aminobutyric acid). This is a calming neurotransmitter that keeps the brain from being overstimulated. Low levels are associated with anxiety. This chemical has been labeled a major chemical involved with learning and memory (Laviv et al., 2010).

Glutamate. This stimulating neurotransmitter activates systems involved in learning and memory.

Norepinephrine. Your brain requires norepinephrine to form new memories and to transfer them to long-term storage. It is the primary excitatory neurotransmitter needed for motivation, alertness, and concentration.

Serotonin. This is a calming neurotransmitter. Serotonin plays an important role in regulating memory and learning, as well as appetite and body temperature. Low serotonin levels produce insomnia and depression, aggressive behavior, and increased sensitivity to pain. In order to pay attention and make good decisions, a balance in this chemical is useful.

☀ **Mental Note: Memories are stored in networks of neurons that communicate chemically through neurotransmitters.**

Searching for Memory

Sensory Memory

All information enters our brains through one of our senses: taste, smell, sight, hearing, or touch. Sensory memories are fleeting. They last seconds or less—just long enough for our brains to recognize what we are experiencing. After the thalamus directs new content to the appropriate association cortex, it returns to the hippocampal area, where the sensations are reunited into the complete incident. Attention to it will allow it to stay in the next memory process, immediate memory (Sousa, 2017).

Immediate Memory

If we pay attention to the incoming sensory information, we can hold onto it for about 20 seconds. This memory process is sometimes referred to as *conscious memory* or *short-term memory*, but we really have two short-term memory processes, immediate and working.

This memory practice allows us to look up the number to a restaurant and hold that number in our minds long enough to get it dialed. If we are interrupted in the process, the number slips our mind, and we must look it up again. Immediate memory stores up to seven bits of information for those 20 or so seconds.

Active Working Memory

Taking information from immediate memory and working with it encompasses this memory process. Working memory provides the time and space to manipulate information that is needed for complex cognitive tasks (Baddeley, 1999). Increasing the capacity of working memory helps students perform better on standardized tests (Klein & Boals, 2001). Often long-term memories are brought into working memory to supply prior knowledge that may be associated with the new material. Working memory can hold information for hours, days, or even weeks. In order for information to make it to long-term memory, it must become meaningful in some way. In other words, connections have to be made in the brain between the new material and previously stored material.

In school, our students use working memory as they are solving math problems, answering essay questions, and reading stories and texts. They hold and manipulate pieces of information to create new ideas, formulate hypotheses, and solve problems.

Long-Term Memory

Information that becomes a detailed representation in memory is considered a permanent memory. This type of memory is lasting. It occurs when networks in our brains are created and used often enough that activation occurs easily and the information can be retrieved.

What happens with brand-new information? What if there is no prior knowledge? This is a question I am often asked. New material can be stored in long-term memory via different pathways. Perhaps putting information to music or movement will help store it. Adding a strong emotional component may make the difference between forgetting and remembering. Sometimes pointing out similarities and differences between certain kinds of information can help make sense out of it and allow it to be stored.

To perform complex cognitive tasks, our students must maintain access to large amounts of knowledge. There are large demands on working memory during activities such as text comprehension and skilled performance, so that the usual representation of working memory involving just temporary storage must be extended to include working memory based on information previously stored in long-term memory. For example, a student reading a story must have access to previously mentioned characters and scenarios for proper references for pronouns. The student also needs contextual information to integrate logically the information presented in the current sentence with the text previously read. Similarly, in mathematical calculations, the student must maintain the results of transitional steps in memory (i.e., mental math problems). Long-term memory and working memory interact at these times.

Long-term memory can be separated into two types of memory: explicit and implicit. Then these types of memory can be further divided into specific kinds of memory (see Figure A.5).

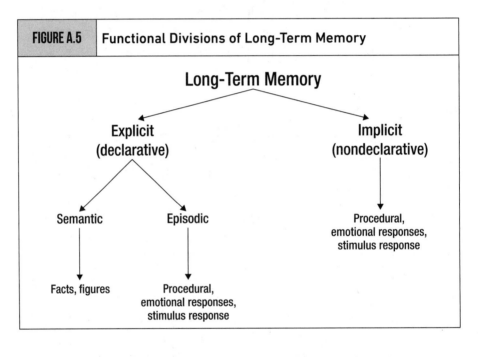

| FIGURE A.5 | Functional Divisions of Long-Term Memory |

Long-Term Memory

Explicit (declarative)

Implicit (nondeclarative)

Semantic

Episodic

Procedural, emotional responses, stimulus response

Facts, figures

Procedural, emotional responses, stimulus response

☀ **Mental Note: Memory must go through several different processes to become permanent.**

Explicit Memory

Explicit memory is exercised when performance on a task requires conscious remembrance of previous experience (Sousa, 2017). It may be easier to relate this type of memory if you think of it as *direct* memory (Baddeley, 1999). Explicit memory consists of long-term memories that are consciously learned. This includes semantic and episodic memory. Both are learned through the same brain structure, the hippocampus, yet they are very separate types of memory. The hippocampus appears to repeatedly play patterns of information, gradually training the appropriate area of cortex to acquire permanent memory.

The differences between episodic and semantic memory are notable for educators. According to Tulving (1999), *episodic* memory implies remembering, whereas *semantic* memory implies knowing. Remembering always involves knowing, but knowing does not necessarily imply remembering. We can use both these memory pathways to help our students succeed and raise achievement levels. Both pathways can be influenced by multimodal experiences. They are each accessible through a variety of retrieval routes.

Because semantic and episodic memory both involve the knowledge of facts—both can be brought to mind, and both can be declared—they are sometimes called *declarative* memory (Wolfe, 2010).

Episodic Memory

Tulving (1985) refers to episodic memory as *autonoetic*, which means knowing about yourself. This type of memory refers to locations and descriptions of events and people. Episodes, if you will, have a story effect—a beginning, a middle, and an end. They are memories that are distinct in time and space. We can consciously remember past experiences. Episodic memory is stored through the hippocampus. It catalogs these events, experiences, and locations.

A study of London cab drivers gives evidence of how we can change the brain and add memories. To become a London cabbie, one must study for two years. Cabbies' brains were scanned at the start and end of this period, and the results showed the hippocampi of the drivers increased over the two years. With more experience driving, their brains continued to change (Brown, 2011).

Episodic memory is context-related. Results of studies show us that when we learn something in a specific location, we will recall it better in that same location (Baddeley, 1999).

Semantic Memory

Semantic memory is *noetic*, or knowing. Semantic memories are not necessarily time- or space-related, but are context-free knowledge of facts, language or concepts. They are also stored through the hippocampus. This structure is too small to store all our semantic memories, so it feeds the information to the proper area of the neocortex. This process takes some time (and some sleep!). The hippocampus also makes note or catalogs the information, so that the memory can be easily retrieved. Most researchers believe that at some point the hippocampus is not necessary to access the memory. Through a special process, memories become accessible without this pathway; however, it can take days, months, or even years for this to occur (Wiltgen et al., 2010).

Semantic memory is not learned all at once; it is learned through repetition. This is information that we learn; once it is learned, we generally forget how or when we learned it.

☀ **Mental Note: The educational system utilizes explicit memory most of the time.**

Implicit Memory

Implicit memory is sometimes referred to as *nondeclarative memory*. Rather than the intentional learning that is explicit, implicit learning is incidental or nonconscious. It is *indirect* learning (Baddeley, 1999). Some of these memories began explicitly but through repetition became implicit. In other words, we do something procedural, like driving the car, but do not consciously draw to mind the instructions for doing so. Besides procedural knowledge, implicit memory includes emotional responses, skills and habits, and stimulus responses.

Procedural Memory

This is our "know how" memory. It is timeless and does not involve conscious recollection. Although sometimes called *muscle memory*, procedural memory can be both motor and nonmotor (Levine, 2002). The basal ganglia and the cerebellum are involved in this type of memory.

Sequences that are repeated are stored in this memory pathway. They may be motor procedures, such as riding a bike and tying a shoe, or non-motor procedures, such as telling a story from beginning to end and the sequence of the scientific method.

Saying "please" and "thank you" are habits that we acquired through learning the procedures of good manners.

Emotional Memory

If we look again at the amygdala in the middle of the brain, we can see how close it is to the thalamus. Some say that it is just one neuron away (Goleman, 2013). This implies that the emotional area of our brains receives and filters incoming information quickly—even before it has a chance to go up to the neocortex for higher-level thinking and recognition. Because of this, information that is not neutral will be examined and stored by the amygdala. The amygdala will react to emotional content without our conscious knowledge of it

Stimulus Response

Considered a reflexive memory, the stimulus response is a response to a particular stimulus. It has been compared to the "hot stove" effect. Or, someone sneezes, and your response is "God bless you." When we teach students opposites, they often become "automatic" learning. I say, "Stop"; my students say, "Go." Flash cards and rap songs create this type of learning. Many call this memory system "automatic" (Sprenger, 2010).

Mental Note: Implicit memory may be more powerful and lasting than explicit memory.

Appendix B
Graphic Organizers

FIGURE B.1	Venn Diagram

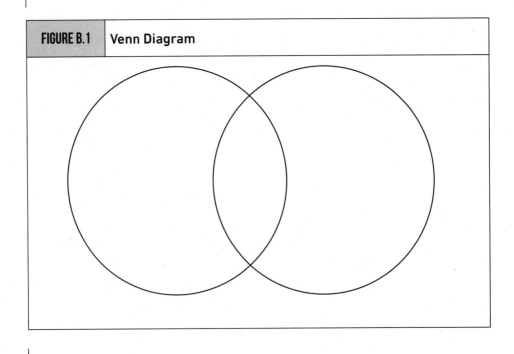

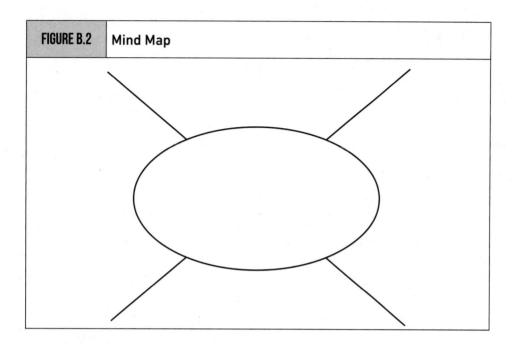

FIGURE B.2	**Mind Map**

FIGURE B.3	**KWHLU Chart**

K	W	H	L	U

Adapted from Ogle (1986)

FIGURE B.4	T-Chart

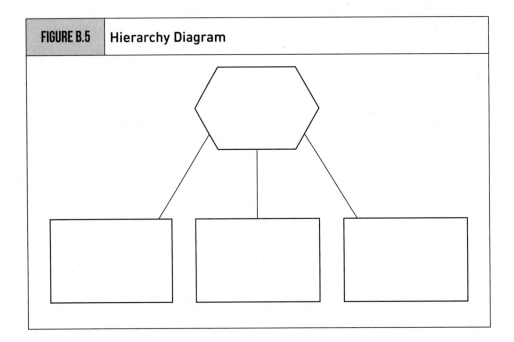

FIGURE B.5	Hierarchy Diagram

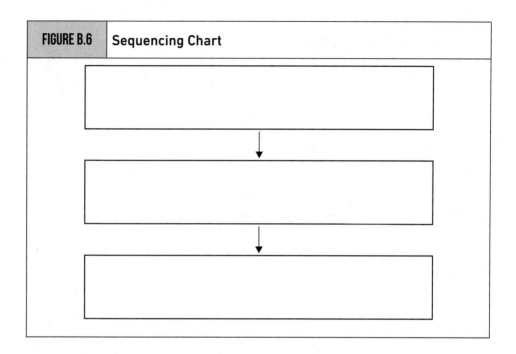

FIGURE B.6	Sequencing Chart

FIGURE B.7   PMI chart

Plus	Minus	Interesting

Plus: What did you understand about the presentation?

Minus: What did you have trouble with? Dislike?

Interesting: What areas would you like to know more about?

FIGURE B.8	Cause-and-Effect Organizer

What Happened?

Because

Because

Because

FIGURE B.9	Cause-and-Effect Map

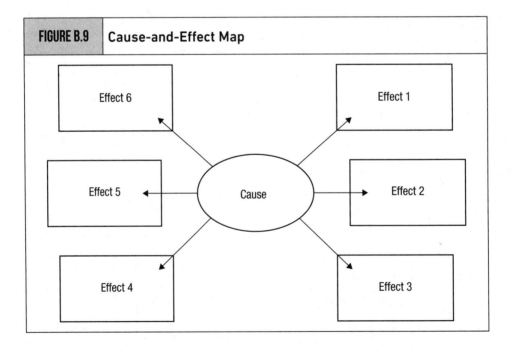

FIGURE B.10 | **Cause-and-Effect Chain**

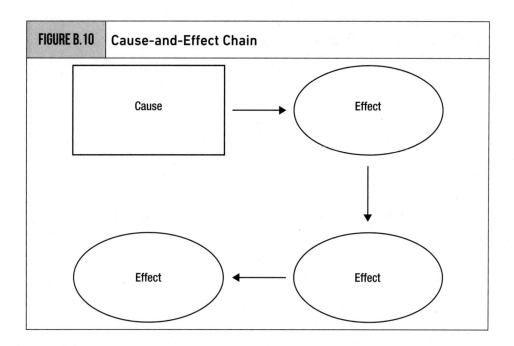

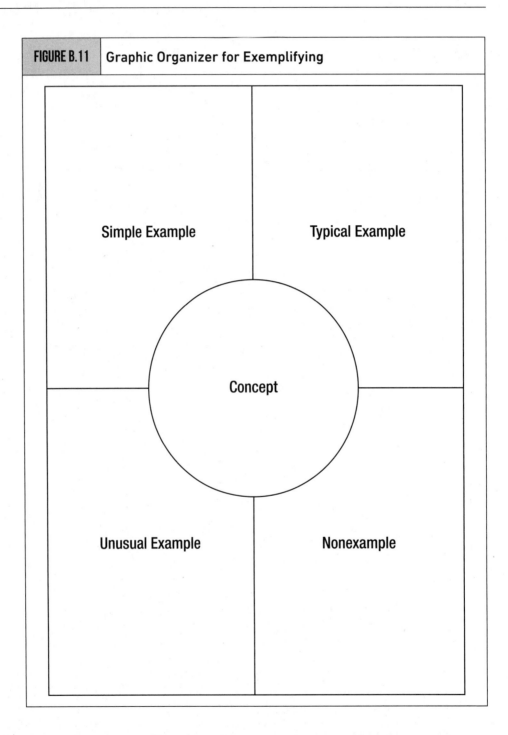

FIGURE B.11   Graphic Organizer for Exemplifying

Simple Example

Typical Example

Concept

Unusual Example

Nonexample

References

ACT, Inc. (2016/17). *Test preparation.* Available: http://www.act.org/content/act/en/products-and-services/the-act/test-preparation.html.

Alber, R. (2014, January 15). How important is teaching literacy in all content areas? *Edutopia.* Available: https://www.edutopia.org/blog/literacy-instruction-across-curriculum-importance

Allday, R. A., Bush, M., Ticknor, N., & Walker, L. (2011). Using teacher greetings to increase speed-to-task engagement. *Journal of Applied Behavior Analysis, 44*(2), 393–396.

Allen, R., & Scozzi, N. (2012). *Sparking student synapses, grades 9–12: Think critically and accelerate learning.* Thousand Oaks, CA: Corwin.

Anderson, J. R. (2000). *Learning and memory: An integrated approach* (2nd ed.). New York: Wiley.

Anderson, L., Krathwohl, D., Airasian, P., Cruikshank, K., Mayer, R., Pintrich, P., et al. (Eds.). (2001). *A taxonomy for learning, teaching, and assessing.* New York: Longman.

Andreason, N. (2004). *Brave new brain.* New York: Oxford University Press.

Armstrong, T. (1993). *Seven kinds of smart.* New York: Plume.

Armstrong, T. (2016). *The power of the adolescent brain: Strategies for teaching middle and high school students.* Alexandria, VA: ASCD.

ASCD Research Brief. (2004, May 25). Retention and student achievement. Available: http://www.ascd.org/publications/researchbrief/v2n11/toc.aspx

Atkins, S., & Murphy, K. (1993). Reflection: A review of the literature. *Journal of Advanced Nursing, 18*(8), 1188–1192.

Baddeley, A. (1999). *Essentials of human memory.* East Sussex, United Kingdom: Psychology Press.

Bailey, F., & Pransky, K. (2014). *Memory at work in the classroom: Strategies to help underachieving students.* Alexandria, VA: ASCD.

Bednark, J. G., Campbell, M. E. J., & Cunnington, R. (2015). Basal ganglia and cortical networks for sequential ordering and rhythm of complex movements. *Frontiers in Human Neuroscience, 9,* 421.

Benjamin, N. (2010). "People think in stories" presentation. Available: http://csuepress .columbusstate.edu/csu_tv/159

Biffle, C. (2013). *Whole-brain teaching for challenging kids.* Yucaipa, CA: Whole Brain Teaching, LLC.

Bloom, F., Beal, M. F., & Kupfer, D. (Eds.). (2003). *The Dana guide to brain health.* New York: Dana.

Boud, D., Keough, R., & Walker, D. (1985). *Reflection: Turning experience into learning.* London: Kogan Page.

Brookhart, S. (2017, January 26). How to give effective feedback to your students. [ASCD Webinar.] Available: http://www.ascd.org/professional-development/webinars/how-to -give-effective-feedback-to-your-students-webinar.aspx

Brophy, J. (1987, October). Synthesis of research on strategies for motivating students to learn. *Educational Leadership, 45*(2), 40–48.

Brown, M. (2011). How driving a taxi changes London cabbies' brains. *Wired.* Retrieved from https://www.wired.com/2011/12/london-taxi-driver-memory/

Bruning, R. H., Schraw, G. J., & Ronning, R. (1999). *Cognitive psychology and instruction.* Upper Saddle River, NJ: Prentice-Hall.

Burke, K. (2009). *How to assess authentic learning* (5th ed.). Thousand Oaks, CA: Sage.

Burmark, L. (2002). *Visual literacy: Learn to see, see to learn.* Alexandria, VA: ASCD.

Burns, M. (2012). The new brain science of learning. [Video.] Available: https://www.youtube .com/watch?v=ahSYwchh-QM

Burrows, D. (1995). The nurse teacher's role in the promotion of reflective practice. *Nurse Education Today, 15*(5), 346–350.

Butler, R. (1987). Task-involving and ego-involving properties of evaluation: Effects of different feedback conditions on motivational perceptions, interest and performance. *Journal of Educational Psychology, 79*(4), 474–482.

Cahill, L. (2004). *Ten things every educator should know about the amygdala.* Presentation at the Winter Learning Brain Expo, San Diego, California.

Caine, R., & Caine, G. (1994). *Making connections: Teaching and the human brain.* Alexandria, VA: ASCD.

Carter, E. W., Wehby, J., Hughes, C., Johnson, S. M., Plank, D. R., Barton-Arwood, S. M., et al. (2005). Preparing adolescents with high-incidence disabilities for high-stakes testing with strategy instruction. *Preventing School Failure, 49,* 55–62.

Chapman, C., & King, R. (2000). *Test success in the brain-compatible classroom.* Tucson, AZ: Zephyr.

Chapman, C., & King, R. (2012). *Differentiated assessment strategies: One tool doesn't fit all* (2nd ed.). Thousand Oaks, CA: Corwin.

Chappuis, J., Stiggins, R., Chappuis, S., & Arter, J. (2011). *Classroom assessment for student learning: Doing it right—Using it well* (2nd ed.). London: Pearson.

Cohen, J. (1999). *Educating minds and hearts.* Alexandria, VA: ASCD.

Colbert, B., & Knapp, P. (2000, October 18). *This sucks. You're stupid: Giving negative feedback.* Paper presented at the William Mitchell College of Law, Midwest Clinic Conference.

Comer, J. (2003). Transforming the lives of children. In M. Elias, H. Arnold, & C. Hussey (Eds.), *EQ + IQ = Best leadership practices* (pp. 11–22). Thousand Oaks, CA: Corwin.

Connellan, T. (2003). *Bringing out the best in others.* Austin, TX: Bard Press.

Cooke, V. (1991). *Writing across the curriculum: A faculty handbook.* Victoria, Canada: Centre for Curriculum and Professional Development.

Costa, A., & Kallick, B. (2000). *Describing 16 habits of mind.* Retrieved from: http://www.habits ofmind.net/pdf/16HOM2.pdf

Costa, A., & Kallick, B. (Eds.) (2009). *Learning and leading with habits of mind: 16 essential characteristics for success.* Alexandria, VA: ASCD.

Cotton, K. (2000). *The schooling practices that matter most.* Alexandria, VA: ASCD.

Covey, S. (1989). *The seven habits of highly effective people.* New York: Simon & Schuster.

Crannell, A. (1994). *Writing in mathematics with Dr. Annalisa Crannell.* Available: https://www. fandm.edu/uploads/files/107682389602454187-guide-to-writing.pdf

Crew, J. (1969, Spring). The effect of study strategies of the retention of college text material. *Journal of Reading Behavior, 1*(2), 45–52.

Crossland, R., & Clarke, B. (2002). *The leader's voice: How your communication can inspire action and get results!* New York: Select Books.

Crowley, K., & Siegler, R. (1999, March–April). Explanation and generalization in young children's strategy learning. *Child Development, 70*(2), 304–316.

Damasio, A. (1999). *The feeling of what happens.* New York: Harcourt Brace.

Danielson, C. (2002). *Enhancing student achievement: A framework for school improvement.* Alexandria, VA: ASCD.

Danielson, C. (2011). *The framework for teaching evaluation instrument.* Hoboken, NJ: The Danielson Group.

Dean, C., Hubbell, E., Pitler, H., & Stone, B. (2012). *Classroom instruction that works: Research-based strategies for increasing student achievement* (2nd ed.). Alexandria, VA: ASCD.

DeFina, P. (2003). *The neurobiology of memory: Understand, apply, and assess student memory.* Presentation at the Learning and the Brain Conference, Cambridge, Massachusetts.

Dehn, M. (2010). *Long-term memory problems in children and adolescents.* Hoboken, NJ: Wiley.

Desautels, L. (2016, March). How emotions affect learning, behaviors, and relationships. *Edutopia.* Available: https://www.edutopia.org/blog/emotions-affect-learning-behavior -relationships-lori-desautels

Dewey, J. (1910/1997). *How we think.* New York: Dover.

Dickman, M., & Blair, N. (2002). *Connecting the brain to leadership.* Thousand Oaks, CA: Corwin.

Diekelmann, S., & Born, J. (2010). The memory function of sleep. *Nature Reviews Neuroscience, 11*(2), 114–126.

Dunlosky, J., Rawson, K. A., Marsh, E. J., Nathan, M. J., & Willingham, D. T. (2013). Improving students' learning with effective learning techniques. *Promising Directions from Cognitive and Educational Psychology, 14*(1), 4–58.

Dweck, C. (2006). *Mindset: The new psychology of success.* New York: Random House.

Eichenbaum, H., & Dickerson, B. (2010). The episodic memory system: Neurocircuitry and disorders. *Neuropsychopharmacology, 35*(1), 86–104.

Engle, R. W., Kane, M. J., & Tuholski, S. W. (1999). Individual differences in working memory capacity and what they tell us about controlled attention, general fluid intelligence, and functions of the prefrontal cortex. In A. Miyake & P. Shah (Eds.), *Models of working memory: Mechanisms of active maintenance and executive control* (pp. 102–131). Cambridge: Cambridge University Press.

Erlauer, L. (2003). *The brain-compatible classroom: Using what we know about learning to improve teaching*. Alexandria, VA: ASCD.

Feldman, R. (2007). On the origins of background emotions: From affect synchrony to symbolic expression. *Emotion 7*(3), 601–611.

Fogarty, R. (2003). *Nine best practices that make the difference*. Thousand Oaks, CA: Corwin.

Fogarty, R. (2009). *Brain-compatible classrooms* (3rd ed.). Thousand Oaks, CA: Corwin Press.

Francis, E. (2016). What EXACTLY is Depth of Knowledge? (Hint: It's NOT a wheel!) *ASCD Edge*. Available: http://edge.ascd.org/blogpost/what-exactly-is-depth-of-knowledge-hint-its-not-a-wheel

Gardner, H. (1983). *Frames of mind: The theory of multiple intelligences*. New York: Basic Books.

Gazzaniga, M. (1999). *The mind's past*. Berkeley: University of California Press.

Gelb, M. (1998). *How to think like Leonardo da Vinci*. New York: Dell.

Giannetti, C. G., & Sagarese, M. (2001). *Cliques: Eight steps to help your child survive the social jungle*. New York: Broadway.

Glasser, W. (1999). *Choice theory*. New York: Perennial.

Goldberg, E. (2001). *The executive brain: Frontal lobes and the civilized mind*. New York: Oxford University Press.

Goleman, D. (1998). *Working with emotional intelligence*. New York: Bantam.

Goleman, D. (2013). *Focus: The hidden driver of excellence*. New York: HarperCollins.

Gordon, B., & Berger, L. (2003). *Intelligent memory*. New York: Viking.

Gregory, G., & Kaufeldt, M. (2015). *The motivated brain: Improving student attention, engagement, and perseverance*. Alexandria, VA: ASCD.

Guillory J., Hancock, A., & Kramer, J. (2011). Upset now? Emotion contagion in distributed groups. *Proc ACM CHI Conference on Human Factors in Computing Systems* (Association for Computing Machinery, New York), 24, 745–748.

Hamann, S. B., Ely, T., Grafton, S., & Kilts, C. (1999). Amygdala activity related to enhanced memory for pleasant and aversive stimuli. *Nature Neuroscience, 2*, 289–293.

Harris, M. T. (2014). The effects of a test-taking skills intervention on test anxiety and test performance on 4th graders. [Thesis paper.] http://digitalcommons.lsu.edu/cgi/viewcontent.cgi?article=4205&context=gradschool_theses

Harvey, S., & Goudvis, A. (2007). *Strategies that work* (2nd ed.). York, MN: Stenhouse.

Hattie, J. (2012). Know thy impact. *Educational Leadership, 70*(1), 18–23.

Hattie, J., & Yates, G. (2014). *Visible learning and the science of how we learn*. New York: Routledge.

Hamid, A. A., Pettibone, J. R., Mabrouk, O. S., Hetrick, V. L., Schmidt, R., Vander Weele, C. M., Kennedy, R. T., Aragona, B. J., & Berke, J. D. (2016). Mesolimbic dopamine signals the value of work. *Nature Neuroscience 19*(1), 117–126.

Higbee, K. (1996). *Your memory: How it works and how to improve it*. New York: Marlowe.

Holzer, M. L., Madaus, J. W., Bray, M. A., & Kehle, T. J. (2009). The test-taking strategy intervention for college students with learning disabilities. *Learning Disabilities Research and Practice, 24*, 44–56.

Jensen, E. (2013). *Engaging students with poverty in mind: Practical strategies for raising achievement.* Alexandria, VA: ASCD.

Jensen, E., & Nickelsen, L. (2008). *Deeper learning: 7 powerful strategies for in-depth and longer-lasting learning.* Thousand Oaks, CA: Corwin.

Johnson, D. (2001). *Critical issue: Beyond social promotion and retention—Five strategies to help students succeed.* Available: http://www.readingrockets.org/article/beyond-social-promotion-and-retention-five-strategies-help-students-succeed

Johnson, D., Johnson R., & Holubec, E. (2007). *The nuts and bolts of cooperative learning* (2nd ed.) Minneapolis, MN: Interaction Book Company.

Johnson, N. L. (1995). *Active questioning: Questioning still makes the difference.* Beavercreek, OH: Pieces of Learning.

Johnson, S. C., Baxter, L. C., Wilder, L. S., Pipe, J. G., Heiserman, J. E., & Prigatano, G. P. (2002). Neural correlates of self-reflection. *Brain, 125*(8), 1808–1814.

Kahn, P. (2002). *Advice on using examples of ideas.* Retrieved from http://www.palgrave.com/skills4study/html/subject_areas/maths/maths_ideas.htm

Keeley, M. (1997). *The basics of effective learning.* [Unpublished manuscript.] Available: http://www.bucks.edu/~specpop/memory.htm

Kemmis, S. (1985). Action research and the politics of reflection. In D. Boud, R. Keogh, & D. Walker (Eds.), *Reflection: Turning nursing into learning* (pp. 139–163). London: Kogan Page.

Kenyon, G. (2002). Mind mapping can help dyslexics. *BBC News.* Retrieved from http://news.bbc.co.uk/1/hi/education/1926739.stm

Kerry, S. (2002). Memory and retention time. *Educationreform.net.* Retrieved from http://www.education-reform.net/memory.htm

Kihlstrom, J. (2011, March 8). How students learn—and how we can help them. Paper presented to the Working Group on How Students Learn. Retrieved from http://socrates.berkeley.edu/~kihlstrm/GSI_2011.htm

Klein, K., & Boals, A. (2001). Expressive writing can increase working memory capacity. *Journal of Experimental Psychology: General, 130*, 520–533.

Kohn, A. (1993). *Punished by rewards: The trouble with gold stars, incentive plans, As, praise, and other bribes.* New York: Houghton Mifflin.

Kolb, B., & Whishaw, I. (2009). *Fundamentals of human neuropsychology.* New York: Worth.

Kuczala, M. (2015). *Training in motion: How to use movement to create engaging and effective learning.* New York: AMACOM.

Küpper-Tetzel, C. E., Kapler, I. V., & Wiseheart, M. (2014, July). Contracting, equal, and expanding learning schedules: The optimal distribution of learning sessions depends on retention interval. *Memory and Cognition, 42*(5), 729–741.

Laviv, T., Riven, I., Dolev, I., Vertkin, I., Balana, B., Slesinger, P. A., & Slutsky, I. (2010). Basal GABA regulates GABA(B)R conformation and release probability at single hippocampal synapses. *Neuron, 67*(2), 253–267.

LeDoux, J. (2002). *Synaptic self.* New York: Viking.

Lengel, T., & Kuczala, M. (Eds.). (2010). *The kinesthetic classroom: Teaching and learning through movement*. Thousand Oaks: Corwin.

Levine, M. (2002). *A mind at a time*. New York: Simon & Schuster.

Levine, M. (2003). *The myth of laziness*. New York: Simon & Schuster.

Marsh, R. (2013). *Storytelling in education: imagery arts—foundation of intelligence and knowledge*. Available: https://mazgeenlegendary.wordpress.com/storytelling-in-education

Marzano, R. (1998). *A theory based meta-analysis of research on instruction*. Aurora, CO: Mid-continent Regional Educational Laboratory.

Marzano, R. J. (2007). *The art and science of teaching*. Alexandria, VA: ASCD.

Marzano, R. J. (2017). *The new art and science of teaching*. Bloomington, IN: Solution Tree; and Alexandria, VA: ASCD.

Marzano, R., & Kendall, J. (1996). *Designing standards-based districts, schools, and classrooms*. Alexandria, VA: ASCD.

Marzano, R., Pickering, D., & Heflebower, T. (2010). *The highly engaged classroom*. Bloomington, IN: Solution Tree.

Marzano, R. J., Pickering, D. J., Norford, J., Paynter, D., & Gaddy, B. (2001). *A handbook for classroom instruction that works*. Alexandria, VA: ASCD.

Marzano, R. J., Pickering, D. J., & Pollack, J. (2001). *Classroom instruction that works*. Alexandria, VA: ASCD.

Marzano Center Staff. (2013). *Have you done your homework on homework? Marzano Model stresses timing and quality* [blog post]. Available: http://www.marzanocenter.com/blog/article/have-you-done-your-homework-on-homework-marzano-model-stresses-timing-and-q/

Marzano Center Staff. (2015). *Four types of questions that increase rigor* [blog post]. Available: http://www.marzanocenter.com/blog/article/four-types-of-questions-that-increase-rigor/

Maslow, A., & Lowery, R. (Eds.). (1998). *Toward a psychology of being* (3rd ed.). New York: Wiley.

Mason, D., & Kohn, M. (2001). *The memory workbook: Breakthrough techniques to exercise your brain and improve your memory*. Oakland, CA: New Harbinger.

Mateika, J., Millrood, D., & Mitru. G. (2002). The impact of sleep on learning and behavior in adolescents. *Teachers College Record, 104*(4), 704–726.

Mazza, S., Gerbier, E., Gustin, M., Kasikci, Z., Koenig, O. Toppino, T., et al. (2016). Relearn faster and retain longer: Along with practice, sleep makes perfect. *Psychological Science, 27*(10), 1321–1330.

McGee, P. (2017, February 14). Help students reflect and set goals for powerful learning. *Corwin Connect Newsletter*. Available: http://corwin-connect.com/2017/02/help-students-reflect-set-goals-powerful-learning/

McNeil, F. (2009). *Learning with the brain in mind*. Thousand Oaks, CA: Corwin.

McTighe, J., & Wiggins, G. (2013). *Essential questions: Opening doors to student understanding*. Alexandria, VA: ASCD.

Medina, J. (2014). *Brain rules: 12 principles for surviving and thriving at work, home, and school*. Seattle, WA: Pear Press.

Merriam-Webster Collegiate Dictionary. (2003). (11th ed.). Springfield, MA: Merriam-Webster.

Moss, C. M., & Brookhart, S. M. (2009). *Advancing formative assessment in every classroom: A guide for instructional leaders.* Alexandria, VA: ASCD.

Mueller, C. M., & Dweck, C. S. (1998). Intelligence praise can undermine motivation and performance. *Journal of Personality and Social Psychology, 75,* 33–52.

National Education Association. (2003). *Balanced assessment: The key to accountability and improved student learning.* Retrieved from http://www.assessmentinst.com/pdfs/nea -balancedassess.pdf

Northwest Regional Educational Laboratory (NWREL). (2002). *Research you can use to improve results.* Originally prepared by Kathleen Cotton, NWREL, Portland, OR, and published by ASCD in 1999.

O'Connor, K. (2009). *How to grade for learning, K–12* (3rd ed.). Thousand Oaks, CA: Corwin.

Ogle, D. (1986). The K-W-L: A teaching model that develops active reading of expository text. *The Reading Teacher, 39,* 564–570.

O'Keefe, P. A. (2014, September 5). Liking work really matters. *The New York Times.* Retrieved from https://www.nytimes.com/2014/09/07/opinion/sunday/go-with-the-flow.html

Olivier, C., & Bowler, R. (1996). *Learning to learn.* New York: Fireside.

Panskepp, J, & Biven, L. (2012). *The archaeology of mind: Neuroevolutionary origins of human emotions.* New York: Norton.

Pappas, P. (2010, January 4). *A taxonomy of reflection: Critical thinking for students, teachers, and principals.* Available: http://peterpappas.com/2010/01/taxonomy-reflection-critical -thinking-students-teachers-principals-.html

Paul, R. (1993). *Critical thinking: How to prepare students for a rapidly changing world.* Santa Rosa, CA: Foundation for Critical Thinking.

Pearson, P. D., & Gallagher, M. C. (1983). The instruction of reading comprehension. *Contemporary Educational Psychology, 8,* 317–344.

Perkins, D. (1995). *Outsmarting IQ.* New York: Free Press.

Perry, B. (2016, January 20). A child's brain needs experience, not just information. *Smarter Parenting.* Available: http://www.smarterparenting.com/blog/single/A-childs-brain -needs-experience-not-just-information

Pinker, S. (1999). *How the mind works.* New York: Norton.

Popham, W. J. (2001). *The truth about testing: An educator's call to action.* Alexandria, VA: ASCD.

Rabinowitz, J. C., & Craik, F. I. M. (1986). Specific enhancement effects associated with word generation. *Journal of Memory and Language, 25,* 226–237.

Ramirez, G., & Beilock, S. L. (2011, January 14). Writing about testing worries boosts exam performance in the classroom. *Science, 331*(6014), 211–213.

Ratey, J. J., with Hagerman, E. (2008). *Spark: The revolutionary new science of exercise and the brain.* New York: Little, Brown.

Restak, R. (2000). *Mysteries of the mind.* Washington, DC: National Geographic.

Richards, R. (2003). *The source for learning and memory strategies.* East Moline, IL: Linguisystems.

Rogers, S. (2013). *Teaching for excellence* (5th ed.). Evergreen, CO: Peak Learning Systems.

Rothstein, D., & Santana, L. (2011). *Make just one change: Teach students to ask their own questions.* Boston: Harvard University Press.

Rowe, M. B. (1973). *Teaching science as continuous inquiry.* New York: McGraw-Hill.

Rowe, M. B. (1986). Wait time: Slowing down may be a way of speeding up. *Journal of Teacher Education, 37*(1), 43–50.

Sandi, C. (2013). Stress and cognition. *WIREs Cognitive Science, 4*(3), 245–261.

Sapolsky, R. (2012). *The psychology of stress.* [Video.] Available: https://www.youtube.com/watch?v=bEcdGK4DQSg

Schacter, D. (1996). *Searching for memory.* New York: Basic Books.

Schacter, D. (2001). *The seven sins of memory.* New York: Houghton Mifflin.

Schenck, J. (2000). *Learning, teaching, and the brain.* Thermopolis, WY: Knowa.

Schenck, J. (2011). *Teaching and the adolescent brain: An educator's guide.* New York: W. W. Norton & Co.

Schmoker, M. (1999). *Results: The key to continuous school improvement* (2nd ed.). Alexandria, VA: ASCD.

Senge, P., Cambron-McCabe, N., Lucas, T., Smith, B., Dutton, J., & Kleiner, A. (2000). *Schools that learn.* New York: Doubleday.

Sevener, D. (1990, January). Retention: More malady than therapy. *Synthesis, 1*(1), 1–4.

Shaywitz, S. (2003). *Overcoming dyslexia.* New York: Knopf.

Sinek, S. (2014). *Leaders eat last: Why some teams pull together and others don't.* New York: Penguin.

Singer-Freeman, K. (2003). *Working memory capacity: Preliminary results of research in progress.* [Unpublished manuscript.] Retrieved from http://www.ns.purchase.edu/psych/faculty/freeman.html

Small, G. (2003). *The memory bible: An innovative strategy for keeping your brain young.* New York: Hyperion.

Smith, A. M., Floerke, V. A., & Thomas, K. (2016). Retrieval practice protects memory against acute stress. *Science, 354*(6315), 1046.

Sommer, W. (2010). *Procrastination and cramming: How adept students ace the system.* Available: http://www.tandfonline.com/doi/abs/10.1080/07448481.1990.9936207

Sousa, D. A. (2015). *Brain-friendly assessments: What they are and how to use them.* West Palm Beach, FL: Learning Sciences International.

Sousa, D. A. (2016). *How the special needs brain learns* (3rd ed.). Thousand Oaks, CA: Corwin.

Sousa, D. A. (2017). *How the brain learns* (5th ed.). Thousand Oaks, CA: Corwin.

Sprenger, M. (1999). *Learning and memory: The brain in action.* Alexandria, VA: ASCD.

Sprenger, M. (2002). *Becoming a wiz at brain-based teaching.* Thousand Oaks, CA: Corwin.

Sprenger, M. (2003). *Differentiation through learning styles and memory.* Thousand Oaks, CA: Corwin.

Sprenger, M. (2010). *The leadership brain for dummies.* New York: Wiley & Sons.

Sprenger, M. (2013). *Teaching the critical vocabulary of the common core: 55 words that make or break student understanding.* Alexandria, VA: ASCD.

Sprenger, M. (2017). *101 strategies to make academic vocabulary stick.* Alexandria, VA: ASCD.

Squire, L., & Kandel, E. (2008). *Memory: From mind to molecules* (2nd ed.). Englewood, CO: Roberts and Company.

Stahl, R. J. (1994). *Using think-time and wait-time skillfully in the classroom*. ERIC No. EDO-SO-94-3.

Sternberg, R., Grigorenko, E., & Jarvin, L. (2001, March). Improving reading instruction: The triarchic model. *Educational Leadership, 58*(6), 48–52.

Stickgold, R., & Walker, M. P. (2013). Sleep-dependent memory consolidation. *Nature Neuroscience, 16*(2), 139–45.

Stiggins, R. (2001). *Student-involved classroom assessment* for learning (3rd ed.). Columbus, OH: Merrill–Prentice Hall.

Stiggins, R. (2004). *Student-involved classroom assessment* for learning (4th ed.). Columbus, OH: Merrill–Prentice Hall.

Stiggins, R. (2017). *The perfect assessment system*. Alexandria, VA: ASCD.

Stronge, J. (2007). *Qualities of effective teachers* (2nd ed.). Alexandria, VA: ASCD.

Szpunar, K. K., Chan, J. C. K., & McDermott, K. B. (2009). Contextual processing in episodic future thought. *Cerebral Cortex, 19*, 1539–1548.

Takeuchi, T., Duszkiewicz, A., Sonneborn, A., Spooner, P., Yamasaki, M., Watanabe, M. et al. (2016, September 15). Locus coeruleus and dopaminergic consolidation of everyday memory. *Nature, 537*, 357–362.

Tate, M. L. (2016). *Worksheets don't grow dendrites: 20 instructional strategies that engage the brain*. Thousand Oaks, CA: Corwin.

Teaching in the Fast Lane. (2017, January 26). Six strategies for reteaching. Available: http://www.classroomtestedresources.com/2017/01/6-strategies-for-reteaching.html

Tileston, D. (2000). *Ten best teaching practices*. Thousand Oaks, CA: Corwin.

Tileston, D. (2004). *What every teacher should know about effective teaching strategies*. Thousand Oaks, CA: Corwin.

Tileston, D. (2011). *Closing the RTI gap: Why poverty and culture count*. Bloomington, IN: Solution Tree.

Tileston, D., & Darling, S. (2009). *Closing the poverty and culture gap: Strategies to reach every student*. Thousand Oaks, CA: Corwin.

Tobin, K. (1987, Spring). The role of wait time in higher cognitive level learning. *Review of Educational Research, 57*(1), 69–95.

Tomlinson, C. (2014). *The differentiated classroom: Responding to the needs of all learners* (2nd ed.). Alexandria, VA: ASCD.

Tovani, C. (2000). *I read it but I don't get it: Comprehension strategies for adolescent readers*. Portland, ME: Stenhouse.

Tuckman, B. W. (1998). Using tests as an incentive to motivate procrastinators to study. *Journal of Experimental Education, 66*, 141–147.

Tulving, E. (1985). How many memory systems are there? *American Psychologist, 40*, 385–398.

Tulving, E. (1999). Episodic vs. semantic memory. In R. Wilson & F. Keil (Eds.). *The MIT encyclopedia of the cognitive sciences*. Cambridge, MA: MIT Press.

Vacha, E., & McBride, M. (1993, March). Cramming: A barrier to student success, a way to beat the system, or an effective learning strategy? *College Student Journal, 27*(1), 2–11.

Van Blerkom, D.L. (2011). *College study skills: Becoming a strategic learner*. Boston: Wadsworth-Cengage.

van der Kleij, F. M., Feskens, R. C. W., & Eggen T. J. H. M. (2015). Effects of feedback in a computer-based learning environment on student outcomes: A meta-analysis. *Review of Educational Research, 85*(4), 475–511.

Verhoeven, S., & Boersen, G. (2015). *Move forward with dyslexia! Dismiss the label, dissolve fear of failure, discover your intelligence, deserve success.* CreateSpace.

Wellington, B. (1996). Orientations to reflective practice. *Educational Research, 38*(3), 307–315.

Wenglinsky, H. (2002, February 13). How schools matter: The link between teacher classroom practices and student academic performance. *Education Policy Analysis Archives, 10*(12).

Wheatley, M. (2004). *Simple conversations.* Presentation at the ASCD Annual Conference, New Orleans.

Wiggins, G., & McTighe, J. (2005). *Understanding by design* (2nd ed.). Alexandria, VA: ASCD.

Wiliam, D. (2011). *Embedded formative assessment.* Bloomington, IN: Solution Tree.

Williams, A. (2015, July). 8 successful people who use the power of visualization. Mindbody green.com. Available: https://www.mindbodygreen.com/0-20630/8-successful-people -who-use-the-power-of-visualization.html.

Williamson, A. (1997, July). Reflection in adult learning with particular reference to learning-in-action. *Australian Journal of Adult and Community Education, 37*(2), 93–99.

Willingham, D. T. (2004). The privileged status of story. *American Educator.* Available: http:// www.aft.org/periodical/american-educator/summer-2004/ask-cognitive-scientist

Willis, J. (December 2009/January 2010). How to teach students about the brain. *Educational Leadership, 67*(4). Available: http://www.ascd.org/publications/educational-leadership/dec09/vol67/num04/How-to-Teach-Students-About-the-Brain.aspx

Willis, J. (2012, July 27). A neurologist makes the case for teaching teachers about the brain [blog post]. Available: https://www.edutopia.org/blog/neuroscience-higher-ed-judy-willis

Wiltgen, B. J., Zhou, M., Cai, Y., Balaji, J., Karlsson, M. G., Parivash, S. N., Li, W., & Silva, A. J. (2010). The hippocampus plays a selective role in the retrieval of detailed context memories. *Current Biology, 20*(15), 1336–1344.

Wolfe, P. (2010). *Brain matters: Translating research into classroom practice* (2nd ed.). Alexandria, VA: ASCD.

Wormeli, R. (2014) *Smart homework: Can we get real?* Available: https://www.middleweb .com/16590/smart-homework-can-talk/

Zull, J. (2002). *The art of changing the brain: Enriching the practice of teaching by exploring the biology of learning.* Sterling, VA: Stylus.

Index

The letter *f* following a page number denotes a figure.

About the Author

Marilee Sprenger is an international consultant in educational neuroscience, memory, differentiation, reading, and vocabulary. A former classroom teacher, she began applying brain research in her own classroom beginning in 1992 after attending an Eric Jensen workshop that changed her life. Jensen invited her to travel and train with him so she could present his work. State school boards immediately sought her knowledge, and Sprenger taught during the school year and trained others every summer, weekends, and holidays. During these years, she received her master's degree in curriculum and instruction, specializing in the brain and learning. Through years of experience and research, she began to write books on brain-compatible teaching, differentiated instruction, and learning and memory. She has authored 12 books on the brain and learning, written numerous articles, and has DVDs, webinars, a quick reference guide, and online courses available through ASCD.

Sprenger has extensive experience in elementary, middle, and high school settings, as well as colleges and universities. She has worked with state boards of education providing professional development to other professional development consultants, superintendents, principals, and teachers. Her keynote and workshop competence makes her a sought-after speaker for schools, districts, educational service centers, regional offices of education, and educational conferences.

Applying her knowledge of learning and memory, recent research, and her classroom experiences to state and national standards, she has written several books on teaching academic vocabulary. Her personal "war on word poverty" drives her desire to provide teachers with the best hands-on and minds-on strategies to increase student vocabulary, focusing on native speakers, English learners, students from poverty, and all students who are striving to read and comprehend.

As a member of the American Academy of Neurology, Sprenger is constantly kept informed about the latest brain research applications. Sprenger's research-based, hands-on approach to professional development leaves educators with dozens of strategies to implement immediately in the classroom.

You can reach her at (309) 264-5820, her website marileesprenger.com, by e-mail at brainlady@gmail.com, or on Twitter @MarileeSprenger.

Related Resources

At the time of publication, the following resources were available (ASCD stock numbers in parentheses).

Print Products

101 Strategies to Make Academic Vocabulary Stick by Marilee Sprenger (#117022)

Teaching the Critical Vocabulary of the Common Core: 55 Words That Make or Break Student Understanding by Marilee Sprenger (#113040)

Vocab Rehab: How do I teach vocabulary effectively with limited time? (ASCD Arias) by Marilee Sprenger (#SF114047)

Memory at Work in the Classroom: Strategies to Help Underachieving Students by Francis Bailey and Ken Pransky (#114005)

The Motivated Brain: Improving Student Attention, Engagement, and Perseverance by Gayle Gregory and Martha Kaufeldt (#115041)

The Power of the Adolescent Brain: Strategies for Teaching Middle and High School Students by Thomas Armstrong (#116017)

Teaching Students to Drive Their Brains: Metacognitive Strategies, Activities, and Lesson Ideas by Donna Wilson and Marcus Conyers (#117002)

ASCD EDge® Group

Exchange ideas and connect with other educators on the social networking site ASCD EDge at http://ascdedge.ascd.org/

ASCD myTeachSource®

Download resources from a professional learning platform with hundreds of research-based best practices and tools for your classroom at http://myteachsource.ascd.org/

For more information, send an e-mail to member@ascd.org; call 1-800-933-2723 or 703-578-9600; send a fax to 703-575-5400; or write to Information Services, ASCD, 1703 N. Beauregard St., Alexandria, VA 22311-1714 USA.